# Advance Praise for *The Reenactments*

"Flynn's determination to better understand his life through the act of writing and remembering has yielded a truly insightful, original work." —*Kirkus Reviews*, starred review

"Eloquent, precise, intense and profoundly moving, *The Reenactments* is a powerful and beautiful story about grief, survival, and making art." —Dani Shapiro, author of *Devotion*

"Some words we associate with good memoirs ('moving'; 'brave'). And there are some—even with the best memoirs—we just don't ('intellectually challenging'; 'formally adventurous'). Nick Flynn's *The Reenactments* is all these things, it is sui generis, it will make you cry. I read this book in a very short time. I won't stop thinking about it for a very long time." —Darin Strauss, author of *Half a Life*

"Maybe only poets should be allowed to write memoirs, because they know that our perception is partial, our recollection is worse, and the world is made of shards and fragments that make patterns but leave gaps and sharp edges. Nick Flynn's excellent new memoir embraces the unknown and unknowable as the very core of our experience." —Rebecca Solnit, author of *A Field Guide to Getting Lost*

"Not only are films themselves composed of interiors and exteriors, but their creations are as well. I've never read a book that has captured this fact so precisely, so movingly. The familiar hierarchies are reordered. Flynn has by now fashioned his own world of language, within which he can perform feat after revelatory feat." —Joshua Cody, author of *[sic]*

# THE REENACTMENTS

**BOOKS BY NICK FLYNN**

*The Captain Asks for a Show of Hands*

*The Ticking Is the Bomb*

*Alice Invents a Little Game and Alice Always Wins*

*Another Bullshit Night in Suck City*

*Blind Huber*

*A Note Slipped Under the Door* (with Shirley McPhillips)

*Some Ether*

# THE
# REENACTMENTS

● ● ●

Nick Flynn

sr· mnrks !

2012 !

W. W. NORTON & COMPANY

NEW YORK  LONDON

For information about permission to reproduce selections from this book,
write to Permissions, W. W. Norton & Company, Inc.,
500 Fifth Avenue, New York, NY 10110

For information about special discounts for bulk purchases, please contact
W. W. Norton Special Sales at specialsales@wwnorton.com or 800-233-4830

Manufacturing by Courier Westford
Book design by Daniel Lagin
Production manager: Julia Druskin

Library of Congress Cataloging-in-Publication Data

Flynn, Nick, 1960–
The reenactments / Nick Flynn. — 1st ed.
    p. cm.
ISBN 978-0-393-34435-6 (pbk.)
1. Flynn, Nick, 1960– 2. Poets, American—Biography. 3. Motion pictures—
Production and direction—Biography. 4. American literature—Adapta-
tions. 5. Flynn, Nick, 1960– Another bullshit night in Suck City. I. Title.
PS3556.L894Z467 2013
811'.54—dc23
[B]
                                                    2012036597

W. W. Norton & Company, Inc.
500 Fifth Avenue, New York, N.Y. 10110
www.wwnorton.com

W. W. Norton & Company Ltd.
Castle House, 75/76 Wells Street, London W1T 3QT

1 2 3 4 5 6 7 8 9 0

*disclaimer:* This is a work of nonfiction which attempts to deal with the unknown. Some names have been changed.

this book is dedicated to Jody Draper
*in memoriam*

& to Paul Weitz, Jonathan Flynn, & Robert De Niro
*with deep thanks*

\* ... stop and listen to the bells. (*Pause.*) And so on. (*Pause.*) Be again, be again. (*Pause.*) All that old misery. (*Pause.*) Once wasn't enough for you. (*Pause.*)

— Beckett, *Krapp's Last Tape*

# ONE

**(2011)** All hushed, seven of us huddle in a kitchen, stare into a monitor. It's about to start. The actress playing my mother (Julianne Moore) stares back at us—she's in the middle of a living room, the room is just behind this wall, but I haven't gone into the living room, not yet. A set of headphones hangs from an empty chair with my name on them—Dan points to them, points to my head. It's only the sixth day of shooting, we are in a house in Queens, the owner rents it out at times for films like this, films that contain flashbacks to 1970s smalltown America. This kitchen—paneling stamped to look like wood, avocado-green refrigerator, seamless linoleum floor that looks like tiny bricks— is perfect. It's supposed to be my childhood home, but we will never step outside this house. Today and tomorrow are all interiors—after that we will be gone. Julianne is soaking wet, having just failed to throw herself into the ocean. Or, rather, having failed to keep herself under the waves after she did. You will know this by the next scene, from the note she will write—I know it already, having read the script, having written the book, having been there the first time around. We are meant to imagine that the ocean is near—walking distance—near enough for her to still be wet, which it was. Julianne stands there, waits, eyes downcast, looking toward the familiar carpet, a version of the wall-to-wall we once had (textured, harvest gold). At *ACTION* she begins to sob, or wail. I think of Saramago's *Blindness*, how no one was there, at the beginning of the universe, God's hands (*hands?*) working the nothingness into the somethingness, yet everyone knows what happened.

**ANTONIO** Damasio, the clinical neurobiologist, in *The Feeling of What Happens*, offers this:

> The neurobiology of consciousness faces two problems: the problem of how the movie-in-the-brain is generated, and the problem of how the brain also generates the sense that there is an owner and observer for that movie. The two problems are so intimately related that the latter is nested within the former. In effect, the second problem is that of generating the *appearance of an owner and observer for the movie within the movie . . .*

I'm sitting on my childhood couch (plaid), in my childhood home (Third Cliff), even though I haven't entered that house in years. If I were fifteen I'd be stoned, and if my mother came in she might be stoned as well. If this were my couch (*is this my couch?*). I ask Tom, who has something to do with set dressing, *Was all this furniture here?* He looks around: *Some of it was.* Here's the new thinking: *the brain creates the mind.* It seems obvious, once you think about it (*In this it resembles all the old thinking*). One way the brain does this, according to Damasio, is by "creating images which are unconscious momentary patterns on sheets of neurons called maps." Unlike our usual map, though, these maps won't really help you to find your way, not out of this. Each is momentary, one small point in the house you've been wandering, lost, all these years.

**HOW** did I end up in Queens, in this house which is not my house, watching a woman who is not my mother (yet somehow is) reenact the last moments of her life? How? I said yes (yet I could have just as easily said no)—it's as simple as that. After all, how often are you offered the chance for a complete reenactment of the day of the disaster? After all, who doesn't feel, at times, like you are watching the movie being made of your life (if only you had just one more take things might have worked out better)? After all, whose childhood home doesn't feel like a prop, until you leave it, then it is the dream you enter, night after night.

The director (Paul Weitz) yells, *CUT*, and a frenzy of activity invades Julianne's solitude—the lights must be adjusted, the camera moved in closer. Hair redampened, makeup retouched. Then someone (not Paul) yells, *SET*, and just as quickly everyone vanishes. At *ACTION* Julianne begins to wail again, but this time in a way that is almost animal—a three-in-the-morning, dying-in-the-woods animal sound. Water drips from Julianne's sleeve onto the carpet. A lamp behind her bleeds light into the living room (strange term, *living room*)—the window beside it, also bleeding.

Anne Carson, in her introduction to her translation of Sophocles' *Electra*, catalogues Electra's various cries throughout the play, each with its own significance. *Let us consider how Electra constructs her screams.* You know the story: Electra's father

19

(Agamemnon) is murdered by her mother (Clytemnestra) and her stepfather (Aegisthus). Electra declares, *I cannot* not *grieve*, and so she wails, rages, laments, despairs.

I think of this as I watch Julianne. I watch each take.

Then it's over—*CUT*. Paul goes to her, I can see them on the screen, he is telling her something—about tears, I imagine—while a woman adjusts her hair. Then someone calls out, *SET*, and everyone, at once, vanishes—my mother is alone again, looking down at the carpet. At *ACTION* she holds herself this time as she sobs, and then she stops, stares into a middle distance for what seems forever (*For the dead, I see, feel no pain*)—*CUT*. The costumer joins her onscreen, wraps a white terry-cloth bathrobe around her shoulders. Then she steps out of the frame of the monitor, and all that remains is an empty room. On her way out, on her way to her trailer, she passes close by me, but I do not reach out, I do not say hi, though we had spoken just yesterday, the first day she was my mother.

**THE** *feeling of what happens*—the last thing my mother's hand would touch was a pen, the last words she would write were, *I feel too much*. She wrote these words, this phrase, three times—

*I feel too much*
*I feel too much*
*I feel too much*

—each letter getting larger as she wrote, until by the last page there was only room for these four words. Then nothing, then silence—no, not silence, no—the last thing her hand would touch wasn't a pen, wasn't a word, wasn't a note, no, that's not right.

**DARK** polyethylene filters are being taped to the windows, making it night. The actor playing me when I'm eleven (Liam Broggy) is sitting beside me on the couch (*this looks nothing like my childhood home*). We're between shots (*this is how poor people live*), the lights are being moved (*except I did have this awful white paneling in my bedroom*), Yesterday, when we first met, Liam told me he wanted to be a writer. I was distracted by his—my, our (the?)—mother (Julianne), who was standing a few feet away, holding a basket of laundry. I hadn't spoken to her yet, I didn't know if I could. She was about to read my notebook, the words I wrote, years ago, a story I was working on, which may or may not have set in motion her suicide. The notebook was hidden, misplaced, behind a pillow on the couch we are now sitting on. Liam asked me, What do you have to do to become a writer? I looked at him (*is this what people mean when they refer to their inner child?*). What do you have to do? You write, to be a writer you have to write. . . . My inner child, and what do I do? I snap, I bark, I'm short. Now I'm trying to make it up to him. I tell him I started out trying to write things that were like what I liked to read—mysteries, science fiction, horror. Philip K. Dick, Vonnegut, Poe.

What do you read? I ask.

● ● ●

**YESTERDAY** was the sixth day of filming, it was Julianne's first day, I knew that, I couldn't help but know it, as the day approached. I couldn't help but think, perversely, that on Wednesday, in two days, I would meet my mother again, after so many years. I even told a friend in Texas, Tomorrow I get to see my mom again, and he looked at me with horror, maybe pity, hard to tell. *On the sixth day God created man and woman and gave them dominion over the fish and the earth and birds and all that crawls and slithers.* On the sixth day God created *the only animal that commits suicide.*

• • •

**THE** neurobiologist Vilayanur (V. S.) Ramachandran, in *A Brief Tour of Human Consciousness*, offers this:

> *One common fallacy is to assume there is an image inside your eyeball, the optical image, exciting photoreceptors on your retina and then that image is transmitted faithfully along a cable called the optic nerve and displayed on a screen called the visual cortex. This is obviously a logical fallacy because if you have an image displayed on a screen in the brain, then you have to have someone else in there watching that image, and that someone needs someone else in his head, and so on ad infinitum.*

Now Paul, like some demented god, leans over Julianne, telling her what to write in her note. Then he takes me aside, asks me if there is anything she could write between the passage where she reads my notebook and the passage where she tells me she tried to throw herself in the ocean. This, I'm learning, is part of the reason I'm here—to fill in the white space hovering around the story of what happened. I take a page and write, "I tried so hard, I wanted everything to be alright."

Perfect, Paul says.

**ASH** Wednesday, the first day of Lent. I wasn't aware our first day with Julianne was Ash Wednesday until one of the women from the office came to set with the little *X* smudged onto her forehead (the thumbprint of the priest). If you're Catholic (I'm not), then you know you're supposed to give something up for Lent—cigarettes, chocolate, porn. It is a period meant, for believers, to be a reenactment of the time Jesus went into the desert—a time of prayer, repentance, almsgiving. Of self-denial. To contemplate, to meditate, to evaporate. To escape, briefly, the cage of ego. Forty days is what we usually say when we talk about Jesus in the desert, but what this means is simply *a long time*—like Noah's rain, like Moses on the mountain. More than a month. Long enough to starve, which is why we give something up—anything—in order to empathize with Jesus, with his sacrifice. Most scholars, though, agree that Jesus must have eaten something in the desert—some berries, some leaves, whatever grew there. Not much, but something. No one goes for forty days without food, not even Christ himself.

**AS** Julianne readies herself for the next take, the line producer (Caroline) touches my thigh, to offer comfort (I guess), but it feels like an electric prod. This morning, when I first got to set, Paul's assistant (Dan) tried to pitch me two ideas for movies—one about a cat who spits up diamonds, the other a homoerotic prison flick. It was, it seemed, his job to distract me—I was only too willing to be distracted. When Julianne stops crying, Paul turns to me, asks if I'm okay, then asks if I have anything for him, by which he means do I have any input on what we are seeing. What I am seeing is my mother on the day of her suicide, a day I've only imagined, end-lessly, not having been with her on that day. I ask if the room has changed in the ten years since yesterday, when Liam played me. It hasn't really, and I'm unsure if it should—it didn't seem our house ever changed. Yesterday Paul took me aside and said I didn't have to come, not on Julianne's days, but where else would I go?

We will be filming for forty days.

I just counted the days out on my calendar.

*IF you have an image displayed on a screen in the brain, then you have to have someone else in there watching that image.* . . . This imagined someone inside our heads, watching the movie in our brains, is known among neurobiologists as the *homunculus*. Some call it *the ghost in the machine*. Almost all neurobiologists believe that there is no homunculus—no one but us inside our heads, in spite of what it may feel like. Yet this feeling, this sensation, brings up what is known as "the hard problem of consciousness"—what is it exactly that creates this feeling of knowing, of watching our lives, self-consciously, as they unfold? Another word for this is *qualia*— the sensation of having a sensation—the sense that there is something separate, or parallel, or outside of, our consciousness, outside of what we think of as "self." Most neurobiologists insist qualia are illusory, wholly generated from within, from chemicals firing between our synapses.

● ● ●

**NOW** the cameraman (Gerard—another tiny god) rides his infernal machine toward Julianne, his eye to the lens. The grips have built a little train track in the living room—the camera is on a little train, and the cameraman sits on his little seat. The camera is inexorable as it pushes in toward her. Julianne sits with a towel around her shoulders—she has read my notebook (the *prop* notebook), she has tried to throw herself into the ocean (the ocean we will never see), and now she is writing her note. Now she is writing what I just wrote.

*ACTION.*

*Throughout my whole life,* Teilhard de Chardin wrote, *during every minute of it, the world has been gradually lighting up and blazing before my eyes until it has come to surround me, entirely lit up from within.* As my mother, as Julianne, writes her note I wonder about fury, *her* fury—is she holding on to the pen, or is the pen holding, propping, her up? It is, perhaps, only at this moment, in seeing this, in being here, that I have allowed myself to wonder about that, about her fury.

**THE** owner of this house, I think his name is John, I saw him yesterday making his way to the basement, where (I hear) he has set up a room entirely dedicated to baseball—signed baseballs in glass cases, baseball bats on the walls, posters of Jeter, framed cards from bubblegum packs, baseball hats, memorabilia. The cameraman tells me I have to go down there to see it, but I never do. John reminds me of my father, the way he inhabits his body—*in* it but not *of* it, like the Jehovah's Witnesses say about their place in the world. I was on my way upstairs as he was heading down. I heard there was a bathroom upstairs, which seemed odd, which seemed somehow not right, that the faucets would actually work here, that the toilet would flush. Isn't this a prop? Isn't this a dream? Where do you piss in your dreams?

ON the way to the airport yesterday, to fly from Texas to here, someone on the radio was talking about a television show from the 1950s called *This Is Your Life*, apparently a prototype for our current reality television. The format was this: someone (usually an average American) would be invited before a studio audience, and one by one the significant figures from his or her life would be paraded out—to tell a short vignette, to have a brief reunion. Always there would be at least one dramatic moment, a wild card— a long-lost love, a missing childhood friend, but occasionally they pushed even deeper. In one episode a woman who had lost her entire family—mom, dad, siblings—in the Holocaust (though they didn't yet call it *the Holocaust*) is reunited with a brother, long considered dead. In another episode a man, a Japanese minister (Kiyoshi Tanimoto), who survived the bombing of Hiroshima, gets to meet one of the U.S. pilots (Robert A. Lewis) of the *Enola Gay*, the plane that carried the bomb (Little Boy). As copilot on the *Enola Gay* that day, it was Lewis who, as he watched the city below him burst into flame, uttered *My god, what have I done?* Lewis had, seemingly, stopped off at a bar before the show—to hear him it seems like he is breaking down, about to break down. The Japanese minister seems calm, the radio tells me—he is there with two women who survived the blast yet got *deformed* by it. By the radiation. By the fallout. By the isotopes. By the half-life.

*IF you have an image displayed on a screen in the brain, then you have to have someone else in there watching that image, and that someone needs someone else in his head, and so on ad infinitum. . . .* And what happens when the images in your head begin to move, first in your dreams, then inside your waking, and then she is standing right in front of you, impossibly, again? What happens when she begins to speak the words you wrote for her to speak, the words that were spoken to you, that you transcribed? What happens when you can sit on the couch in your childhood home and speak to your child-hood self, and all you want to do is warn him not to write, not to write a word, even though you know it will be impossible to stop him?

● ● ●

**IN** *For the Time Being* Annie Dillard offers this: *According to Inuit culture in Greenland, a person possesses six or seven souls. The souls take the form of tiny people scattered throughout the body....*

Hidden behind Julianne, just out of sight of the camera, behind that wall, is the guy that turns the lamp on (Tom), and the guy who found the lamp (Ryan), and the woman who will adjust her hair (Monica). My mother looks utterly alone, but they are lurking around her, just out of sight.

Dillard goes on to note that, in Buddhism, *it is always a mistake to think your soul can go it alone.*

● ● ●

*MY god, what have I done?*

**OR** did the copilot say, *My god, what have* we *done?*

# TWO

**WHEN** an arm or leg is amputated, the patient often continues to vividly feel the presence of the missing limb as a "phantom limb." Most patients with phantom arms feel that they can move their phantoms, but in many the phantom is fixed or "paralyzed," often in a cramped position that is excruciatingly painful. According to Ramachandran, every time the patient attempts to move this "paralyzed" limb, he or she receives sensory feedback that the limb isn't moving. This feedback stamps itself into the brain circuitry (*cells that fire together, wire together*), so that, even though the limb is no longer present, the brain has "learned" that the limb is paralyzed.

**UNTIL** I was about Liam's age, when we would still do things as a family, my mother would drive us into Cambridge, maybe once a year, to go see the animals at the Agassiz. Years later, when I tried to find it, it was difficult—it turns out that it isn't called the Agassiz at all. It's called the Peabody. Or the Peabody Museum of Archaeology and Ethnology. Or the Museum of Comparative Zoology at Harvard. Or the Harvard Museum of Natural History. Even now it's a little confusing—one building bleeds into the next, so what you call it depends upon which door you enter. But, for some reason, we called it the Agassiz. When I asked people in Harvard Square, no one knew what I was looking for, until I said, *The museum with all the stuffed animals.* Then they knew.

**INSIDE,** as I remember it, is room after room of wooden cases, with glass sides and tops, or cases set into the walls with glass fronts. Inside some are dioramas (an eagle fighting a rattlesnake, big-eyed lemurs lined up on branches, a gorilla beating his chest), but most are just the animals themselves, stuffed and looking blankly, or menacingly, out. A lot of birds, so many in each case that it is hard to distinguish one from the other. Appropriately, the birds are kept above the rest, up on a balcony, all four walls lined with glass-fronted cases, and inside the cases the bodies of every bird that ever flew or hopped—their wings pinned open, some with their beaks aiming straight down to the ground, some aiming up, their bodies arranged into patterns, which seems to have little to do with what their lives had been like. A little card next to each, with its Latin name, followed by, what do you call it, its *popular name*? *Zenaida macroura* (mourning dove). *Rynchops niger* (black skimmer). *Grus americana* (whooping crane). Some pinned with their wings open as if in flight, some arranged on a branch as if sleeping. Everything that had ever flown, or at least everything that was flying at the moment they sealed the cases.

• ● ◉

**OF** course, there is also the case displaying the birds that have vanished since the museum started collecting them—now this is our only chance to see them, though they can no longer see us. Step right up: The dodo, the ivory-billed woodpecker (also known as the *Lord God bird*), the great auk. The Eskimo curlew, the spectacled cormorant. Gone.

One theory about our experience of memory is that it is less like a movie (a permanent emulsion of chemicals on celluloid) and more like a play (subtly different each time it's performed). In this view memory arises from a network of cells, stored in various parts of the brain, or even in the body (body memory), constantly being reconsolidated, rewritten, remade, reenacted. Is this still true when the thing we remember now only exists in a glass case marked EXTINCT? Isn't that the one play that is always the same, night after night?

**NIETZSCHE** offers this:

A human being may well ask an animal: "Why do you not speak to me of your happiness but only stand and gaze at me?" The animal would like to answer, and say: "The reason is I always forget what I was going to say"—but then he forgot this answer too, and stayed silent; so that the human being was left wondering.

In some ways all museums of natural history are like stage sets, though as we wander past the corpses it is as if the play has not yet begun, as if it will never begin. In this they are different than zoos, where the animals, though trapped in their sad dioramas, at least contain the potential to break the glass, to rip our throats out.

IN his work with those suffering from phantom limb syndrome, Ramachandran found he could relieve the pain by placing the subject within a specially constructed mirrored box, dividing the body along the breastbone, which reflected the remaining arm (or leg) in such a way that it appeared, to the subject, that his body was whole again. This is what the subject would see, when in the box—his body, his arm, returned. This is what his mind would see, this is the image of himself (whole) that he hadn't seen since the accident, this is the image he'd never stopped seeing. *I always forget what I was going to say.* Ramachandran has discovered phantom limb syndrome among animals as well, yet whether a mirrored box could relieve their symptoms remains inconclusive.

● ● ○

**ONE** room in the Agassiz is darker than the rest—the room of the Glass Flowers—from the outer hallway you cannot see what is inside. Unlike the rest of the museum, where you can wander freely from room to room, you must choose to enter the room of the Glass Flowers, through one of two doors. Inside it is quieter, the air moves slower, the lights dimmed. The cases are placed at waist level, you must lean over, if you are an adult, to read the descriptions, to see the filaments, the petals, the veins in each leaf. If you are a child the cases are at eye level, but you will want to be lifted up, to see the flowers as your mother sees them. But you cannot lean against the glass cases, a guard will insist you back away, insist you simply lean in closer. Inside each case are the flowers, not real but exact replicas, some over a hundred years old, yet each (well, most) petal as bright as when it was pulled (pinched?) from the hot glass. In some ways this is the inverse of the animals in the hallways outside this room—the animals were once alive, and these flowers will never die.

# THREE

**HEADLINE:** *Scientists Use Brain Imaging to Reveal the Movie in Our Mind* (UC Berkeley News, 2011)

*Imagine tapping into the mind of a coma patient, or watching one's own dream on YouTube. Using functional Magnetic Resonance Imaging (fMRI) and computational models, UC Berkeley researchers have succeeded in decoding and reconstructing people's dynamic visual experiences—in this case, watching Hollywood movie trailers.*

*As yet, the technology can only reconstruct movie clips people have already viewed [in the lab]. However, the breakthrough paves the way for reproducing the movies inside our heads that no one else sees, such as dreams and memories, according to researchers.*

*"This is a major leap toward reconstructing internal imagery," said Professor Jack Gallant, a UC Berkeley neuroscientist and coauthor of the study published online today in the journal* Current Biology. *"We are opening a window into the movies in our minds."*

**(2011)** On my phone is a fifty-seven-second video clip of a stretch of sidewalk in an unnamed city—dusk, snow on the ground, the sidewalk glistens wet (*the brain creates the mind by creating images*). An ambulance passes, with its red siren and twisting lights, adding a sense of chaos. Several people walk to or away from the camera, a man on a bicycle comes close and passes. In the last few seconds one man walks toward us, briefly fills the frame, then continues on, so it seems he is the one being filmed all along. He appears, he reads, as homeless—two coats, a paperbag seemingly held together with duct tape, tissue tucked under his hat.

**THE** man walking through the snowy city in the final seconds of the video clip is the actor (Robert De Niro) playing my father in the film version of his—my—life. It was, it became, the first day of shooting, though it was weeks before filming was due to begin, weeks before my mother—Julianne—would show up. They needed my father—De Niro—in the snow, and it was snowing, so Paul threw together a guerrilla crew, and now, now that the filming is done, we can see him, walking beside a snowy graveyard. My father did walk a city (maybe not this city), wrapped in layers of coats, through snowstorms, through freezing rain. He did sleep outside, years on end (at the time it seemed it would never end), nearly losing his toes to frostbite, at least he told me he was losing his toes, when I found him one night, or one of the hundreds of nights I found him, outside. In the film we will hear De Niro in voiceover say, *I am losing my toes to frostbite due to not taking my shoes off at night.* These are the words my father told me, when I found him, or perhaps he wrote those words to me—all I know is that I can still hear them.

●  ●  ●

The snow, in this scene at least, is real.

The snow-covered graveyard is real.

**WE** *are opening a window into the movies in our minds.* Neuroscientists had, a few years earlier, succeeded in reconstructing static visual patterns, such as a black-and-white photograph, by studying brain activity. In the laboratory, strapped into a machine, you (the subject) looked at a black-and-white postcard of, say, a field with a single bare tree in it—the computer wired to your brain was able to spit out a photograph of something that looked like a bare tree in a field. It reconstructed what you saw. What the Berkeley neuroscientists have done is to push it even further, and now they have reconstructed a movie, solely from what happens to the visual cortex as we watch a movie.

**(2005)** Paul Weitz and I meet for the first time at a café in L.A. (Ammo). It's lunchtime, we sit outside, and as we speak I notice, over Paul's shoulder, a guy who is living out of his pickup truck. To most, I'd imagine, he wouldn't read as homeless, yet to me it's obvious. I watch as he subtly sponges his armpits off in his front seat, then he dries himself, pulls on a shirt, steps out, gets a few things out of the back. Checks the meter. Goes for a walk around the block, comes back with a coffee, checks the meter again. His jeans are a little dirty around the pockets, slightly too long, the cuffs stapled up—all of these are signs. I point him out to Paul, I point out the signs. Most of the homeless are like this guy, I say—invisible—my father was like this guy. I tell him that the one thing I don't want is to stereotype "the homeless"—I tell him I could care less how I end up being portrayed.

*I could care less how I end up being portrayed*—is this even true? By saying it am I trying to suggest I've escaped the cage (or is it a zoo?) of my own ego? Unlikely—after all, who talks about how they are to be portrayed in the film version of their life? But it is true that when I catch a glimpse in a mirror I almost never recognize myself, and when I see my name written out it takes me a moment to realize it refers to me. This could all suggest I'm simply lost in my own hall of mirrors, that I haven't escaped anything. *I could care less.* Perhaps what I mean is that at times it seems I barely know myself, so how could I control how anyone else sees me? I simply try to track the things I find myself doing, feeling, the circles my mind orbits, perpetually. In a few weeks, during the filming, red signs will be taped to a staircase of the building meant to be the former strip joint (Good Times) I once lived in, the words NICK'S BED-ROOM printed on them, beneath an arrow pointing up—even as I stand in the doorway I will know enough not to lie in that bed.

**IN** *Incognito* the neuroscientist David Eagleman proposes that we are unknown to ourselves: *Most of what we do and think and feel is not under our conscious control.* Eagleman invokes the German philosopher and psychologist Johann Friedrich Herbart, who introduced a key concept: *There exists a boundary between conscious and unconscious thoughts; we become aware of some ideas and not of others.* Through various experiments in the limits of our powers of perception, Eagleman concludes that we are not perceiving what's out there, we're perceiving whatever our brains tell us is out there. This gets into the argument of whether there is even such a thing as free will, of whether our unconscious impulses determine all or most of our actions, if we are in fact able to make any rational decisions. For most neuroscientists, Eagleman included, the concept of free will is uncomfortably close to the idea of the homunculus, of the ghost in the machine, which drifts into the dangerous realms of what is named *the soul.*

**WHEN** I was Liam's age something (depression?) draped a wet wool blanket over our house—it threatened to suffocate us all, I knew the only way I'd be able to breathe was if I found a way to poke my fingers through it. Virginia Woolf, in *Moments of Being*, offers this: *Behind the cotton wool is hidden a pattern; that we—I mean all human beings—are connected with this; that the world is a work of art; that we are parts of the work of art*, but I hadn't yet read Woolf. In my little cage I could feel the cotton wool push in on me, and the idea that I was simply a small part of a larger pattern, that I could push the cotton wool aside—if briefly—peer out through a finger-sized hole, put my mouth to it, breathe, would have given me hope. Years later Stanley Kunitz would echo Woolf: *I believe very strongly in the web of creation. I think we are all part of it and if we disturb it at any one point, the whole web trembles.*

• • •

I meet another screenwriter in those first few days in L.A.—over the phone he let me know that he's the go-to guy for class issues in Hollywood. At a café we talk a little about how class has been portrayed in American film (*Midnight Cowboy, Coal Miner's Daughter, Norma Rae*), how it died off in the early 1980s. We talk about the way John Travolta, in the opening shot of *Saturday Night Fever*, struts (lopes? parades?) down a Brooklyn sidewalk, swinging a can of paint, using what working-class people have always used— his body. Some American independents go there now: *The Wrestler, Winter's Bone, Blue Valentine, Wendy and Lucy*. Fellini used to go there: think of *La Strada*, or *Nights of Cabiria*. The French still go there: the Dardenne brothers (*La Promesse*), Jacques Audiard (*A Prophet*). Films like *Biutiful*, or *Lilya 4-ever*, or *Gomorrah* still go there. All these films, all these bodies, slowly crushed under the wheel of a brutal system. The Hollywood go-to guy for class issues gives me a lift back to my hotel in his Porsche, and gives me his latest script, which I read on the plane home. The working class as cavemen, it has mine workers literally smearing their own shit on walls, speaking in little more than grunts. *Go.*

**(2011)** That first day, with De Niro in the snow, also happened to be my birthday—my plane flew between snowstorms in from Texas (where I teach) and somehow landed in New York in time for me to see him walking down the snow-filled sidewalk (*here we go again*). The crew is just a handful of people, shuffling the cold off beneath a freestanding art deco clock on lower Broadway. A few I've already met, a few I haven't. I shake everyone's hand, the cinematographer (Declan) says, It's real now. It's my birthday, I tell him. *CUT.* Paul turns to me, asks, You got anything? This is the first time he will ask me this, at first I don't know what he means, then I realize I'm supposed to do more than simply film De Niro on my iPhone. After the next take I tell Paul, Maybe De Niro could be muttering to himself as he walks, telling the story that is keeping him afloat. In the years after he made it off the streets I got to know all my father's stories—the one about robbing banks, the one about him writing his masterpiece, the one about his father inventing the life raft—but back then, when I'd see him like this, shuffling toward the shelter, holding himself against the cold, I had no idea what he was muttering to himself—my mind was full up with my own mutterings.

**EIGHTY** to ninety percent of the known universe is what we call *dark matter*, simply because we do not know what it is. Similarly, what the brain is doing when we are apparently doing nothing (daydreaming, say) has come to be called *dark energy*. Like the universe, this dark energy takes up an enormous amount of what goes on in the brain, and we know almost nothing about it. On the radio I hear a Rumanian mathematician (Mario Livio) being asked if mathematics are invented or discovered—if invented, this suggests that the laws of the universe are inside us, generated wholly from between our synapses (no ghost in the machine). If discovered, then they are outside of us, connected to something larger (what?)—Plato felt that these truths, these natural laws, were out there, and all we do is discover them. Livio gently posits that it is sometimes both, "a complex mixture of invented and discovered." Mathematics explains the physical world, which is definitely outside our consciousness, which in fact created our bodies, which in turn created our minds, our consciousness. Then, like some Ouroboros, it is our consciousness that then either invents (or discovers) the world. Yet, as Livio points out, no matter how much is discovered, or invented, so much is still inexplicable (*the whole web trembles*).

**DARK** matter, dark energy. Beckett, in a letter to a friend about the limits of language, offered this: *Drill one hole after another into it until that which lurks behind, be it something or nothing, starts seeping through.* Or, as my therapist always interrupts me to ask, *What are you feeling right now?*

**SHINJI** Nishimoto, lead author of the Berkeley study (*Scientists Use Brain Imaging to Reveal the Movie in Our Mind*), offers this: *Our memory may be like watching a play, but our natural visual experience is like watching a movie.* If you go online you can see the clip the subject watched, playing beside the clip generated by his brain activity. It is a split screen, the whole thing is twenty-nine seconds long. On the left side is the clip the researchers put together for the subject to view—it's not exactly the trailer for a film, but more of a surrealist collage of images. Steve Martin moving across a living room, then the title of a movie (*All Bets Are Off*), then a blob of what looks like black ink, then back to Steve (this time in *The Pink Panther*), then to elephants walking across a desert, then to a parrot flying, then to an airplane landing, then to a young man with a stethoscope, then to a talking head. On the right side of the split screen is the corresponding film generated by the computer studying the brain activity of the subject as he watched the clip. It is eerie, in that it is almost frame for frame an impressionistic version of the left side of the screen. Steve Martin becomes a blurry talking head, the title sequence generates some unreadable text, the spreading black ink looks like spreading black ink, the elephants are pure motion, the airplane becomes a landscape of light, the parrot is

60

a red-orange smudge, the talking heads are bleary heads. Does this mean that inside us is a film, vague and blurry, of everything we have ever seen? Does this mean that in thirty years we will be able to project our dreams onto the ceiling as we sleep? What does this say about the stories we tell ourselves to keep ourselves afloat?

**THIS** past summer, head to head with my three-year-old daughter on the grass, staring into the blue, she asked me where the sky started. It comes out of us when we breathe, I told her. Then we breathe it back inside us. Now, when I lie with her in her bedroom, before she falls into sleep, she opens her eyes wide in the dim light and points to the ceiling: Do you see that? she asks. That baby bear coming out of its cave? Amazing, I say, the ceiling shadowy white above us. Where is the bear going? I ask. She's going to find her mother, she tells me. O, I say. I'm making that with my eyes, she says. I have magic eyes.

# FOUR

**CONSIDER** the cattle, Nietzsche writes, *grazing as they pass you by. The animal is seemingly happy, or at least content, to stand in a field all day, tearing at the grass.* To understand this, to feel what they feel, we take the longhorn (or the emu, or the Brahmin), empty him out, stuff him with sawdust, and put him in a glass box. And yes (*lord help me*), if I stand before this corpse, with its black glass eye, if I stand in meditative awareness, I can absorb some of its elusive happiness. But the question remains—wouldn't I get more out of standing in awe before a living thing? I worry that this is what we are doing by making this film, that we are attempting to contain the world, to hold it, to understand it. Everything so uncertain now (was it ever not?)—oceans rising, ice caps melting, species vanishing. Yet at this moment, miles to the north, a polar bear is standing over a hole in the ice, waiting for a seal to emerge. He covers his black nose with his own paw, seemingly aware (really?) that his nose is the only thing that makes him visible. Nietzsche didn't know this, he couldn't have, it hadn't yet been observed, that even polar bears, like us, can act on some level of self-awareness.

**COLLECTIVE** *memory* is the term used to describe those memories that are shared by groups. Neurobiologists seem more comfortable calling this concept *memes* (rhymes with *genes*), a word coined by Richard Dawkins. If your group has all watched a particular film, say, then there will be a collective memory of that film. Walter Benjamin, on the idea of collective memory, offers this:

> It is half the art of storytelling to keep a story free from explanation as one reproduces it. . . . The most extraordinary things, marvelous things, are related with the greatest accuracy, but the psychological connection of the events is not forced on the reader. It is left up to him to interpret things the way he understands them, and thus the narrative achieves an amplitude that information lacks.

**THIS** is what I remember: De Niro, at the beginning of *The Godfather, Part II*, moves catlike across the rooftops of Little Italy as a parade winds its way through the streets below. He is tracking the reigning godfather (*Don Fanucci*—I had to look up his name), who, in his long white coat and white hat, walks alongside the parade. De Niro enters a building through a rooftop door, takes a gun out from his belt, and wraps his hand in a white towel. The towel, we all know, is to silence the blast. As he waits in the shadows he practices aiming at the empty door. He waits. We hear Fanucci's footsteps before we see him, we see his white hat rising up from the stairwell, and then he is at his door, looking for the key. De Niro calls out softly, Fanucci turns—is that how it happens, or does Fanucci just sense his presence? The first bullet ignites the towel, it pops into flame, De Niro doesn't seem to notice at first, focused, as we are, on the shock on Fanucci's face as he falls back into his apartment. Then, as an afterthought, De Niro shakes his burning hand—the towel unwraps, the flame goes out.

*I always forget what I was going to say.* I forgot that De Niro unscrews the lightbulb in the hallway, in order to conceal himself. I forgot that Fanucci, as he stands before his door searching for his key, taps the bulb, and it flickers on, revealing De Niro in the shadows behind him. I forgot that this scene was the echo of another scene in a film by . . . is it Bertolucci (*The Conformist?*)? How did I forget all this? Damasio again:

> The images in the consciousness narrative flow like shadows along with the images of the object for which they are providing an unwitting, unsolicited comment. To come back to the metaphor of movie-in-the-brain, they are *within* the movie. There is no external spectator.

According to Damasio, certain objects get imprinted upon the neural maps that constitute what we call our minds—whatever we took in, early on, in childlike wonder, has now become part of our inner subconscious lives. The act of attention has elevated certain images for each of us, so that now we each carry around inside us our own closed image system (I remember the burning hand, but I forget the lightbulb). Was Don Fanucci wearing a white hat or a black hat, I don't remember. I remember that after he shoots him, De Niro climbs back up to the roof, breaks the gun into little pieces, and drops the pieces down not one, but several, chimneys.

I remember the towel, how it burst into flame.

I remember the gun.

I remember how he made it disappear.

● ● ○

**(2011)** Before filming began, in those few weeks when it was still possible for the whole project to fall apart (again), if someone asked me how it was going, I'd show her the fifty-seven-second clip of De Niro walking in the snow. I wouldn't tell her what it was, I'd cue it up and hand her my phone and let her watch it. I did this a few times before I realized it really says nothing—the image is so grainy, so jangled, so out of focus, that it could simply be a stretch of winter sidewalk nearly anywhere. I could be making it all up. *Is that De Niro on the bike?* a few have asked, and so I've taken to pausing it on the one I call De Niro (look, his *Taxi Driver* face) but, really, it could be anyone. I felt, at times, a little pathetic, a little desperate (really, *De Niro* is playing *my father*). The thing is, you can project nearly anything onto these fifty-seven seconds, so I began to tell myself that this pleased me, and that this is the ultimate purpose of why we're here—to create a scrim that others can project onto, so they can actively participate in trying to make meaning out of this, out of everything. . . .

# FIVE

(2006) A few months after our initial meeting at Ammo, Paul calls saying he wants to meet me in Boston, to visit both my father and the shelter (Pine Street) that my father stayed in, off and on, the years he was homeless. The same shelter I'd been working in for three years when he came to our door. Paul has started mapping out the book, and he needs to fill in some details. I fly in from Texas, he flies in from Los Angeles, and we meet at a Dunkin' Donuts around the corner from my father's apartment, the place he moved into from the streets, set up by someone I'd worked with at Pine Street. It's bitter cold, neither Paul nor I are adequately dressed—January, in Boston, and both of us are wearing thin jackets. I've set up the visit to Pine Street, but it's iffy that we will actually find my father. He doesn't have a phone, and he often spends his days wandering the neighborhood. If you saw him, sitting on a bench, talking to himself, a Dunkin' Donuts cup beside him, you might think he was still homeless. I've made this trip to Boston before, come all this way, and failed to track him down. I know most of his haunts, but not all of them.

We ring my father's bell, the buzzer sounds, we push the door open—as always, he lets us into the building without checking to see who it is. My father's apartment is on the edge of one of Boston's priciest neighborhoods, just across Massachusetts Avenue from Back Bay, in a building of mostly subsidized apartments (*paid for by Uncle Sam*, my father proudly proclaims). We step off the elevator and knock on his door. Who is it? he barks, from behind his chain. Inside it is as I knew it would be—cramped, dingy, smelling of sweat, a wet animal smell. It's as if he never really made if off the streets, as if the street followed him inside. I introduce him to Paul. A pleasure to meet you, my father says. He motions for us to sit, gestures toward his (filthy) bed—there is nowhere on it to sit. I push a pile of last year's newspapers to one side, spread a blanket out over the gray sheet, and we sit. This is the way it always is, this is what I imagine Paul wants to see, though it seems even sadder, even shabbier, with him here. Am I really simply letting my father live out his life like this? Do I have a choice?

Part of this visit, I know, is to make sure I didn't just make it all up, that my father actually lived on the streets, that he didn't just have one drink too many one night (like James Frey). Or like that white girl (Margaret Seltzer) who wrote the book about being raised by the Crips, and even hired a black woman to sit in her living room when the *New York Times* came to visit, to play the part of Big Mom, her (fake) foster mother. Here, in the vodka-sodden flesh, is my father.

My father holds forth awhile—there is really no need to ask him any questions, but I try to steer the conversation. I ask him about his time in prison, and he launches into his story about the book he wrote about it. *In my two years behind bars they shuffled me between a dozen prisons*, he tells Paul—*The Merry-Go-Round of Madman Moose. I am Madman Moose.* At some point, I hand him (another) copy of *Another Bullshit Night in Suck City*, the book I wrote about his time on the streets, my days in the shelter, the book the film will be based on—as always, it's as if he is seeing it for the first time. *What a title*, he says with a laugh. I remind him (again) that it is something he said, while he was homeless. *I was always good with titles*, he agrees. I tell him that Paul is a director, that he's going to make a movie based on the book. It will be about about your life, I tell him. My father, seemingly, is not greatly impressed—he's always expected a movie to be made of his life, his life is fascinating, he is trying to tell us about it now. What do you think of that, Paul asks, of a movie being made about your life? My father narrows his eyes. *Only two people can play me*, he says—*it's got to be either Dustin Hoffman or myself. I've given it a lot of thought. Dustin or me.*

Interesting choices, Paul tells him.

It's nearly dark as we leave. I want Paul to get to the shelter in time for dinner, at five. We take a taxi the few blocks through the now-swanky South End to the shelter—it wasn't like this when I worked here. Then, I tell Paul, the whole neighborhood had been abandoned, which was why they put the shelter here. Even as I worked there it started to change—first the artists moved in, then it went gay, and now it is solidly back to being high-end. Except for all the homeless guys still making their way to the shelter, who we are now passing in increasing numbers. I tell the cab driver to stop on the street, so we can walk up the alley with them. At the front door we get in line, allow ourselves to be frisked, just like every-one else. Then I ask to speak to Lyndia, a friend I'd worked with on the floor years ago, when my father had first shown up. Now she's the director—I'd phoned ahead and she'd agreed to show us around.

Inside, Pine Street is even shabbier than I remembered, sadder (like my father's apartment), though maybe it was (again) because I was with Paul. Maybe I was seeing it as I imagined he saw it: *That was where your father sleeps, this is where he slept?* We spend a few hours in the shelter, talking with guests, looking at the showers, the dorms, the clothing room, the cage. We get in line as dinner is being served, sit at a table with everyone else, eat what they eat (creamed chicken over white rice). When I worked here everyone smoked, smoke hung over everyone's head, stuck to our clothes as we sat in our booth after work at Foley's.

My last two years at Pine Street I worked on what we called the Outreach Van—our mandate was to offer services to those homeless folks who, for one reason or another wouldn't—or couldn't—go to shelters. I joined the Van, in part, to get away from my father, who had, for a couple years at that point, been sleeping in the shelter. Outside, in the frigid night air, I felt I could breathe again. Within a few months, though, my father got himself barred from the shelter and ended up sleeping on the streets—I was back where I started. I'd spend my nights driving past a bench, where someone who may or may not have been my father slept (*It is night & it's snowing & starlings fill the tree above us . . .*)—maybe we'd stop, offer a blanket, a sandwich, maybe it wasn't him, maybe it was.

The shift on the Van went from nine at night until five a.m., which I thought was a good idea, because it meant I had less time to get fucked up. I was getting fucked up a lot those days—all the time—mostly on very strong marijuana. Some mornings, after the shift ended, I'd go home with the woman I'd spent the night working alongside—she had her own problems (doesn't every-one?), my father was simply mine. Some mornings I'd go home alone, get high in my apartment as the sun was coming up, then go back out onto the streets and take photographs of the guys I'd seen a couple hours earlier. Earlier I'd stopped by as a worker—now I came again, with my camera this time. All addicts have radar, all the homeless guys knew I used—they knew I was one of them, it was in my eyes. I was off the clock, I told myself, I could do what I wanted. I sat with them and showed them my camera, asked if they minded—they never minded. I'd go home after I finished a roll or two, sleep for a few hours, wake up around noon, lock myself in the darkroom I'd built in the bathroom, spend a few hours bathing in chemicals and shadows, until my shift began again at nine.

It was easier, when high, to take photographs than to write— photography requires focused attention, and I could focus when high, my world in fact was nothing but focused, reduced to a pin-point, to a chunk of hash impaled on a pin. But writing requires both clarity and a willingness to step into the unknown, and there was nothing clear about my days, not then. Getting fucked up every day is about maintaining the status quo—it has nothing to do with change, or the unknown. Yet I felt this need to make something, anything, and so I made photographs—*click click*— then locked myself in the darkroom for the rest of the day. The photographs themselves meant little to me, not then—what I imagined was that one day I'd be able to look through them and they might help me to make sense of who I'd been. They were like the push-ups one does in prison—meant not so much for today, but more for the day of release. Then I read Sontag's *On Photography*. In it she argues that the proliferation of photographic images has begun to establish within people a "chronic voyeuristic relation" to the world around them, that one of the consequences of photography is that the meaning of all events is leveled, made equal. This sounded a lot like what happened inside me when I got high, it sounded like what I was looking for—numb and unaffected, I felt like I'd found a level space where nothing could surprise me, ever again. The medium itself, Sontag warned, fosters an attitude of anti-intervention, that the individual who seeks to record cannot intervene, and that the person who intervenes cannot then faithfully record, for the two aims contradict each other. This troubled me, for though getting high had become a daily routine, as familiar as a photograph of a famine on the front page, some part of me wanted desperately to intervene, in something, to change the way things were. Why else was I working at a shelter? Years later Sontag would (seemingly) soften her position—*No sophisticated sense of what photography is or can be will ever weaken the satisfactions of an unexpected event seized in mid-action by an alert photographer*—but there was no way those words could have saved me, not then. Sontag hadn't written them yet.

At nine everyone who has a bed at the shelter is in bed. Paul and I move outside, help load the Van. Vinnie is now in charge of the Van—he'll be driving tonight. Vinnie is Native American—a Micmac. When I was working the Van in the 1980s he was living on the streets—always a decent guy, but a hardcore drunk. Not hopeless, but nearly so. Now he's clear-eyed, soft-spoken, smiles easily. He knows every hole in the city one could crawl into. The van is nicer than the one we used to drive—I remember spraying starter fluid into the carburetor some frozen nights, flames shooting up from the engine when the key was turned. We load up blankets and sandwiches and coffee, just like we always did. Our thin jackets are not going to help us tonight, and so before we take off I bring Paul into the clothing room—we each borrow a donated coat, which we will return at the end of the night, or hand off to someone else. Then Vinnie drives.

A call has already come in—it's five degrees above zero, a concerned citizen has seen a man facedown on the sidewalk by the library. Paul wonders, sensibly, if the police shouldn't be called. Vinnie steers us down Boylston, and we scan the sidewalk for the guy. Paul and I jump out to look around, and Vinnie gets another call, for a guy in a doorway on Newbury, around the corner. I tell him we want to look around, ask if he can swing by again in a few minutes—there's a chapter in *Suck City* that unfolds here, the first night my father sleeps on the streets, it would be good for Paul and I to retrace his steps. In *Suck City* my father spends the last of his money on some soup and a beer at a favorite haunt, and then makes his way to the library, to write a letter to Ted Kennedy. *The poor and the homeless are our constituents, we both care deeply about the poor and the homeless.* When the library closes he makes his way across the street to the Dunkin' Donuts, where he nurses a coffee until eleven, closing time. I show Paul the library, the Dunkin' Donuts, the bench my father sat on—only so many options. I wasn't with him the first night he slept out, but for years afterward I'd find him, drinking coffee, or writing letters, or sitting at this bus stop, those years it seemed he'd never make it back inside. Paul needs to see the blowers behind the library, where my father ends up sleeping on his first night out (or so I imagined), and so I lead him there. As we approach we see three or four homeless guys, sleeping where they fell, all these years later. When we make it back to the corner where Vinnie left us there is no sign of him or the Van. Paul and I share a moment of slight panic—everything is now closed, and even in our donated coats we are bone-cold. If you drove past, we would really look no different than any other homeless guys, shivering on a corner, waiting for someone to pull up, offer coffee, a blanket, a ride.

Vinnie does finally return, and we ride the Van until dawn. At one point Paul and I are sitting on the floor of an ATM, talking to a homeless guy—Tommy—who had pulled his laden shopping cart in beside him. This is in South Boston, *Southie*, an especially brutal part of the city. When I was working at the shelter I'd been put in the hospital after being jumped by some punks in Southie one night after work. Southie hasn't changed much—we'd just spent an hour talking to a guy who lived near the railroad tracks, who'd seen a friend beaten to death by some kids with baseball bats the week before. As we sit on the floor talking to Tommy, wearing our donated coats, some punks come up to the doors and shake them, banging on the windows, yelling, KILL THE HOME-LESS FAGGOTS. Paul and I, when we first met, had spoken about the stereotype of the dangerous homeless person, and how in reality most of the homeless are utterly vulnerable to the weather, to cops, to violence. Now here we are, squatting on the floor of an ATM, wearing our homeless coats, as a pack of Southie teenagers paw at the windows, threatening to kill us. I genuinely fear for our lives. I couldn't have planned it better.

**THE** first script Paul writes is beautiful—poetic, smart, dark, weird, moving, like the greatest Rumanian art-house movie you never saw. I read it and weep, my agent (Bill) reads it and weeps, my wife (Lili) reads it and weeps. Paul really did it, Lili says, it's amazing. Then she adds offhandedly, Hollywood will never make this movie. Lili's an actress, she knows the business, and, as it turns out, she's right. Three years and two big studios later, after every junior executive has stuck a finger into it, Paul's beautiful script is nearly unrecognizable—I cannot read a page without wincing. Fortunately, within a year the economy will collapse, and the budget will be cut, and Paul will move to a smaller studio (Focus), and be allowed to go back to his original script.

**ONE** small moment in Paul's first script does feel a little off, and we talk about it the next time we meet, at the same restaurant in L.A., a few months after our night on the Van. It is the scene where the "Nick" character (I guess this is how I will have to start referring to myself) stops off at what the voiceover refers to as "my drycleaner's." It is a scene where I am picking up some trashbags full of clothes from my landlord (not my drycleaner, though my landlord did happen to be a drycleaner when he was younger, which is why he has these clothes to donate). I tell Paul that when I was working with the homeless I didn't have anyone I would refer to as "my drycleaner"—in fact, I don't think I ever had anything drycleaned at all. Even now, twenty years later, I've maybe dropped off a couple suits over the years, but it's hardly a regular thing. I don't think I bought any clothes from anywhere but a secondhand store until I was thirty. Most of my friends worked with the homeless, and no one I knew had a drycleaner. Paul grew up in a very different world than I did—his grandfather was John Huston's agent—and he looked at me oddly for a long minute when I told him this.

How'd you get your clothes clean? he finally asked.

# SIX

**FLAMEWORK** is a glassblower's term for how one can transform sand and pigment into, say, a vase or a glass. Or a flower. Leopold Blaschka, describing his own flamework, wrote:

> Many people think that we have some secret apparatus by which we can squeeze glass suddenly into these forms, but it is not so. We have tact. My son Rudolf has more than I have, because he is my son, and tact increases in every generation.

**(1970)** We drive up to the Agassiz for the day, my mother, brother, and I. It must be a Saturday, when my mother isn't working—she must have the day off from the bank, and she won't have to show up for her bartending job until that night. The drive takes an hour, I know this because the drive from Scituate to Boston always takes an hour, more or less. You take the backroads to the highway, then, just before you enter the city, you drive past the Florentine tower of Pine Street, the tower of the original firehouse, the tower the firemen would practice jumping from, before it became a shelter.

**RAMACHANDRAN** found that when a patient with a phantom arm watched another person's intact hand being rubbed, he actually felt his phantom being rubbed—massaging the other person's hand appeared to relieve the pain in the phantom. This is what we know: certain sensory neurons in your brain are activated, they *fire*, when your hand is touched, and a certain proportion of these same neurons (mirror neurons) also fire when you watch another person's hand being touched, as if the neuron were "reading" the other person's mind, or "empathizing." Some claim that these mirror neurons are what separate us from the apes, but this can only be true if you believe that empathy is limited to humans.

• • ◦

**ON** Ash Wednesday we give something up so we can empathize with Jesus, just as we reenact the crucifixion each spring (*these constant resurrections, these passion plays*), so we can witness, again, his suffering. We see it so we can then remember it, seems to be the idea, even though none of us was there the first time around. Think of the Pietà, the mother gazing upon the unimaginable, knowing she only gets these few moments—one take—to feel whatever it is she is going to feel, for eternity. Ideally, through this yearly reenactment, we will find empathy within ourselves for all who suffer and sacrifice. In practice, though, for some, we end up just picking at old wounds, reenacting scenes from the past, trapped on the wheel of suffering (*samsara*), My problem with empathy is, perhaps, one of perspective—each year, on the anniversary of my mother's death, I never put myself in her place, I don't know if I should—painkillers, ocean, gun—I simply return to the place I found myself in, the moment I heard she was dead.

**LEOPOLD** Blaschka and his son Rudolf, of Hosterwitz, Germany (near Dresden), were the creators of the Glass Flowers. Leopold, as a young man, had gone into the family business of producing glass ornaments and glass eyes. Occasionally he would take on a commission for glass replicas of aquatic creatures—anemones, sea slugs, jellyfish—for museums. At one point he even constructed an aquarium in his house, in order to have live specimens from which to work. In 1886 the Blaschkas were commissioned by George Lincoln Goodale, founder of Harvard's Botanical Museum, to create a series of glass specimens of flowers, to be used for research. Three years later they signed on to a ten-year project. It was to be financed by a former student of Goodale's, Mary Lee Ware, and her mother, Elizabeth. When Leopold died, in 1895, Rudolf took over, and would continue creating the glass flowers until his death, in 1939. In those fifty-plus years over 4,300 models of 830 different plant species were made. Most (two-thirds) seem to have been created in the first eight years, when Leopold was still living, yet this might have more to do with ever-increasing levels of difficulty as Rudolph worked his way through the remaining species—a daisy might be less complex to reconstruct than, say, a stalk of wheat. Yet the Blaschkas took on no apprentices and left no heirs—no one has since been able to replicate their artistry and skill. This knowledge died with Rudolf.

**THE** Glass Flowers exhibit has been called "the Sistine Chapel of glasswork"—does this simply mean they are irreplaceable (though this begs the question as to what *is* replaceable)? Does it mean they are at the very height of artistic achievement, that they inspire awe in the viewers? Perhaps we find something cathartic in the apple blossom that looks like nothing but an apple blossom, but what? Perhaps it is simply, *How did a human being* (or even two) *accomplish this?* Perhaps, depending upon your temperament, the question is, *How did God accomplish this, how did he (or she) connect this leaf to this stem?* Or perhaps you simply believe that the plant found a way, just as the father found a way, and taught the son. Or perhaps we wonder why anyone would spend their lives recreating the world around them. Perhaps this forces us to ask ourselves, in this dimly lit room, how we spend our days. Go, listen to the murmured comments of those in the dark beside you: *None of these are real? Is it possible? Completely glass?*

● ● ●

**THE** Ware mother and daughter employed the Blaschka father and son to gather together all the flowers of the world, impossibly, into one room (*Couldn't one simply visit a greenhouse?* one might ask, though only a greenhouse in a Borgesian fable could contain all the plants in the world). What did these women hope to achieve, what did they want? What kept them going, for fifty years, through one world war, right to the edge of another? Why flowers (not actual flowers, but replicas)? Was it simply a Victorian impulse, the belief that the world could be catalogued, preserved? Did they want to understand this one aspect of the world, to praise it? Were they thrilled by the uncanny illusion each flower offered, how impossible it was to tell which was real, which created? What about the desire to freeze time itself? Decay, rot, death, delayed forever? Was it vanity, to possess the world, or humility, the chance that they could be part of something larger than themselves? What was the original impulse to say yes? Which flower did they first hold in their hands (lilac? hydrangea?) that inspired them to say, Yes, we will do this? Did they see (like I can't help but see) the deeply sexual nature of each flower, opening, offering herself?

● ● ●

**DIDION** offers this: *Time passes. Memory fades, memory adjusts, memory conforms to what we think we remember.* It is possible we went to the Agassiz only once, I know this, this is the way memory works, at least my memory, even if it doesn't feel that way, even if now, when I return, it all seems so familiar, as if I'd spent many hours, many days, there. The walls of birds, the bones of a whale hanging from the ceiling, reassembled into a whale, the cabinet of apes, each seemingly staring straight at me—familiar, yet strange. Ernst Jentsch defined the uncanny as being a product of "intellectual uncertainty, so that the uncanny would always, as it were, be something that one does not know one's way about in." Uncomfortably strange or uncomfortably familiar. Tacked to my bedroom wall in the house I grew up in was a postcard from the cabinet of apes, bought in the Agassiz gift shop. It somehow survived all the purges (white paneling, Fleetwood Mac), right through the time I left that house. Maybe memory is constructed of merely this—a postcard tacked to a wall—maybe this postcard is why the Agassiz is, to me, so familiar, so strange.

# SEVEN

**FOR** the last four summers my wife and child and I have lived in a 150-year-old barn in upstate New York. I renovated it four years ago, putting in just enough work so we could spend the warm months sleeping in it. One night, when Maeve was one and a half, our second summer in the barn, an hour or so after she'd finally drifted off into sleep, the light in her room suddenly switched on (her door is made up of glass panes covered with a thin fabric)— then it switched off. Then on. Then off. On. Off. For the next half hour this continued. I crept to the window—Maeve was standing in her crib, reaching out to the switch, then looking around the room as it snapped into light, aware that she was the one controlling it. She'd only learned to walk a few months earlier.

Her room, from a distance, pulsed like a huge firefly.

● ● ◦

**ANOTHER** true story: I went to a museum in Houston a few months ago, with a friend, a writer who hopes to write a memoir. We were standing before a Maurizio Cattelan sculpture (*All*, 2007)—thirteen bodies covered with thirteen spotlessly white sheets, lined up on the floor at our feet. As we moved in silence slowly around the bodies, we saw that one of them appeared to have had his head cut off, yet it was placed back in the spot where the head should be. Another was missing a hand. Then we realized that each was carved out of its own single block of marble. My friend asked me if it had been cathartic, to write my memoir. I looked down at the sculptures—it was cathartic for me to look at them, but I could imagine it might have been hell to make them (*I was cheered | when I came first to know | that there were flowers also | in hell*). No, I answered—how was it for you to read it?

Aristotle, in his *Poetics*, never promised catharsis for the makers of art, only for the audience. To return to the scene of the crime, or the scene of the death, can take a toll (*and god forgive me, | I pulled to the side of the road and wrote this poem*), but then so does the energy it takes to avoid it, to deny that you are, once again, standing over the corpse, or listening to her laugh in the next room. When I first started out I wrote a series poems about my mother's suicide—at the time it seemed I would never write about anything else (*the good news is the same as the bad news*). Some were purely elegiac, yet they were stuck in a sort of two-step in the seven stages of grief—stuck somewhere between disbelief and rage. When I return to that scene now (reluctantly, ambushed), my experience is not one of catharsis, but of a nearly unbearable resurgence of chaos and pain. And ultimate failure—that container, those poems, can never contain this grief, nor her death, nor does it make anything right, nor does it put it behind me, not forever. *Grief,* as Kevin Young says, *is evergreen.* The urn that holds the ashes might be hand-carved, but the ash will always turn to paste in your throat.

**MAEVE** wakes up some mornings now, when it's still dark out, sobbing. *Hot Pepper*, she cries, *come back, please. Hot Pepper, come back.* Hot Pepper is her little brother, who lives in Paris, who drives a car with his hands and feet out the window, who has ears big enough to hear everything we say, even if we whisper. Maeve is almost four, she has been talking about—and to—Hot Pepper for almost two years now. Sometimes Hot Pepper has fifteen brothers, including Crunch-Crunch and Bailey, sometimes he lives on the head of an elephant, sometimes Paris is the lit windows behind our Brooklyn apartment. Hot Pepper lives there, she tells me, pointing. That's Paris. If she hears a story about anyone who is bad, or mean, she assures us that Hot Pepper will take care of him—Hot Pepper will fly in and knock him down, she promises. *I love Hot Pepper*, she says. I pick her up when she misses him, hold her as she cries. *I know, love, I know*, I murmur—*it's hard to miss someone.*

**PAUL** Levy offers this:

Instead of an *either/or* universe, where our projections are either real or unreal, there is an area in-between in which they are *both/and*: both real and unreal at the same time. Instead of the assumption that our projections are merely unreal figments of imagination, Jung points out their very real effects by saying, "Whatever their reality may be, functionally at all events they behave like realities." Having very real effects, the products of imagination are not imaginary illusions. Jung elaborates, "What we are pleased to call illusion may be for the psyche an extremely important life-factor, something as indispensable as oxygen for the body—a psychic actuality of overwhelming significance. Presumably the psyche does not trouble itself about our categories of reality; for it, everything that *works* is real."

● ● ●

(2010) A few months before we may or may not begin filming (rumors, whispers)—at this point I'm not allowing myself to believe it's real. The anniversary of my mother's death is coming around again, and for some reason it's hitting me hard—harder than last year. I'm having a rough go of it, wrapped in my cotton wool. Catharsis? I know nothing of catharsis. If Lili is out for the night, Maeve will sometimes cry out, *Mommy, come back, Mommy, come back*, over and over. I sit on the couch, stare at the wall, listen to her cry. Mommy come back. Countless hours of therapy have led me to this—her body refuses to stay ash. How to let go? I'm still afraid of being left, and so I dream up escape routes, I believe everyone does, it's barely worth mentioning. Some days I swear that if a woman held out her hand to me I would take it, I would leave my wife and child, I would burn down the house, just so that I would be the one to leave this time. I go to my therapist, I tell him about my struggles, we do some work. I am once again adrift in a sea of incomprehensibility—I will never understand my mother's suicide. For some reason the weight of it, this time around, is crushing. Its intensity seems not to have diminished one watt since the gunshot, so many years ago. My therapist has me lie flat on my back, reach up into the nothingness above me, say the exact words Maeve says. Come back. Don't go.

Afterwards, as I bicycle away, Central Park on my left, I come

100

to Columbus Circle, which is, as always, crowded, frenetic. I'm a little spacey. A woman jumps in front of my bike, holding a small red sign up to me, which I cannot make out. *Get out of the movie*, she yells. I slow down, look around. Movie? It looks like I am simply in New York on a Saturday morning. It seems impossible—is everyone else in the whole city in this movie except me? I look around for the cameras, the lights, anything. *Get out of the movie*, she yells again.

# EIGHT

**IN** *Magnolia*, Julianne Moore enters a drugstore to fill a prescription, ostensibly for her husband, who is dying of cancer, but the pharmacist thinks she is trying to scam him for drugs. He thinks she's an addict, or maybe her character just thinks he thinks this, it's unclear. It seems like she might be scamming, or at least taking a swig of the liquid morphine now and then, or perhaps she is simply distraught, to be so close to death; either way, she goes off on him, in a way that is chilling and complicated, because no one seems to know at that moment what is real. If Julianne, looking for her *motivation*, asked her director, Am I trying to scam the drugs or am I distraught? perhaps the director simply shrugged— all possible scenarios are sometimes true.

**THE** real appearing unreal, the unreal appearing real—this is the definition of the uncanny. Jimmy Stewart, in *Vertigo*, enters deeply into this realm—he loses his mind after witnessing what he believes to be the suicide of his newly beloved Madeleine (Kim Novak). After he is released from the psych hospital he sees a woman—Judy—who reminds him of Madeleine. What he doesn't know is that Judy is Madeline—she was hired to play the role of Madeleine, by the husband who threw the real Madeleine's body from the tower. In the most chilling scene in the film (for me), Stewart gets Judy to dress like Madeleine, to change the color of her hair, to wear it the same way: It can't matter to you, he barks, lost in the depths of his obsession. This obsession feels both real and utterly hopeless, this desire to recreate what has been lost.

**(2011)** I'm on the phone with Julianne, a month before we start filming, we're on speakerphone with Paul. They are, well, I don't know where they are—I imagine a hotel room, maybe a restaurant—just voices without bodies, asking questions about my mother. I say hi to Julianne, say how happy I am she is involved, that I look forward to meeting her. Paul says, Do you have time to talk? I'm outside a bike shop, about to buy a bike (mine was recently stolen)—I have time. So your mother shot herself? he asks. I didn't just make that up, did I? No, you didn't make that up. Where'd she get the gun? he asks. We had lots of guns around my house, I tell him. Some antique ones hung on the wall, a working shotgun in a zippered bag in the closet, the shells in my mother's top drawer. I'd sometimes put them into the gun when she wasn't around, but I don't tell Paul this, nor do I tell Julianne. I don't know why I don't tell them—maybe because my mother didn't know (at least I thought she didn't know), so Julianne doesn't need to know (or maybe she knows already). I tell them she had her own pistol, a .38, which she got a permit for in 1972. I would go target shooting with her, and then later I'd shoot a rifle with my stepfather, the Vietnam vet, and then some other guns with my friends, who were into guns—guns, motorcycles, and beer (and Mink DeVille). I liked the motorcycles and the beer (and Mink DeVille), though I wasn't that into the guns. I tell them that after she died the cops came and took all the guns away, confiscated them. That I never went to retrieve them.

**WHAT** exactly are we, am I, getting into? What I mean is—is this film, will it be, more glass flower, or stuffed ape? That is, am I hoping to take something that was (my mother, her death) and present it as I'd hoped it would be? Or am I taking something that was, and making something out of it that will last forever? Am I reenacting a—her—death, or am I hoping to bring her back? Will Julianne embody my mother, or will my mother embody Julianne? Am I here to try to line up the physics of the world, to recreate what happened, as accurately as possible, in the hope of releasing some hidden energy, in the hope of finding a hinge that will open a door to some truth as yet uncovered? Edgar Morin writes: *There are two ways to conceive of the cinema of the Real: the first is to pretend that you can present reality to be seen; the second is to pose the problem of reality.* The problem of reality? I always thought the problem was, simply, within me.

**IN** 1990, the Iranian director Abbas Kiarostami released *Close-Up*, his half-documentary, half-staged recreation of the real-life trial of a man (Hossein Sabzian) who impersonated a famous Iranian filmmaker (Mohsen Makhmalbaf). In the film, as in life, Sabzian convinces a (rich) family that they will star in his next film (which they will also finance)—eventually they end up having him arrested. Kiarostami reenacts the meeting of Sabzian and the wife on a bus, using the real people. In this initial meeting Sabzian comes off as somewhat innocent—a man from a lower class with artistic aspirations who is mistaken for a famous director. The woman approaches him, mistakes him for Makhmalbaf. All Sabzian does is agree to go to the woman's home for lunch, to meet her family—her son, she tells him, is studying film. All he has to do is say yes. Isn't this what anyone who calls himself an artist has to do, for years before one actually makes anything worthwhile? One has to pretend to be a poet years before one actually is a poet. My father calls himself the greatest writer America has yet produced, we will hear De Niro comparing himself to Salinger and Twain in the opening shot of the film. My first book wasn't published until I was forty, I spent years calling myself a poet with nothing to show for it. If someone had mistaken me for a real poet in those years, can I say I would have contradicted her? Kiarostami reenacts Sabzian's initial discussions with the family, over lunch, in the actual family home. Did he simply set up his camera, bring Sabzian back in, ask them to do what they had done? The son, it turns out, has little interest, at least in this reenactment, in being a filmmaker. Now he wants to be a baker. Some days or weeks pass, the film is beginning to take shape, and then the police come and take Sabzian away. I am unsure, but it seems as if Kiarostami used actual footage from the trial, though perhaps this is recreated as well. At the end of *Close-Up*, Sabzian is released from prison after some months, and Kiarostami films him meeting the real Makhmalbaf. It's devastating—Sabzian breaks down, utters the following, to both apologize for, and to justify, his actions: *Everyone loved me when I was Makhmalbaf.*

**ON** the phone Julianne asks, though it is hard for me to hear, about pills: Which pills did your mother take? I tell her about the Darvon, which I don't even know if they still make, but I believe it was a barbiturate—a knockout pill, a down—she took them for her migraines. Julianne says, O, my mother had migraines too, and I say, O. How old was your mother when she had you? Julianne asks, and I say she was twenty, twenty-one, and Julianne says, My mother was twenty when she had me, and I say, O, yes, so you know, but even as I say the words I don't know what they mean. She asks about her depression and I say, It was mostly just when she had migraines that she'd go inside, that she'd spend a day in bed, that other than that she was vivacious, young, alive. She made it to work every day, and then she went to her other job at night. She didn't miss work, until maybe near the end, when she started doing cocaine and things got a little sloppy. Everyone was doing cocaine then, I add, and Julianne laughs. She got a little off the rails but not so far off. I am leaning over a wrought-iron railing, looking into a restaurant—a Chinese man comes to the window, looks up at me.

**SIMONE** Weil offers this:

> To lose someone: we suffer because the departed, the absent, has become imaginary and unreal. But our desire for him is not imaginary. We have to go down into ourselves to the abode of desire which is not imaginary. Hunger: we imagine kinds of food, but the hunger itself is real: we have to fasten on to the hunger. The presence of the dead person is imaginary, but his absence is very real: henceforward it is his way of appearing.

Paul plans Julianne's scenes—which are all flashback—to be filmed in such a way that they appear washed out, faded, yellowed. Your mother is the specter hanging over every scene, Paul tells me—her presence, her death, is what animates the living.

Does that sound right? he asks.

**WHAT** I don't tell Julianne is this: I remember a lot of orange pill bottles around our house, my mother would save them, perhaps to get them refilled, perhaps to keep track, her top drawer rattled with them. Behind the pill bottles was her gun, alongside a copy of Henry Miller, *Sexus, The Rosy Crucifixion*—this was the drawer where the action was. At some point, when I was around Liam's age, I began taking the pill bottles, stuffing them with firecrackers. I'd cut a little hole into the white childproof caps with an x-acto knife, run the braided fuses through it, to make my little bombs. I'd aim the gun out the window at passing cars, *bang*, I'd make the noise with my mouth. I'd thumb through the Miller and jerk off. Later still I'd simply take the pills themselves, *to see how far they could take me.*

● ● ●

**THE** *problem of reality, the problem of the truth*. I only half understand why I am part of all these conversations. I don't know what else Paul needs to know—he has my book, everything is in the book. He's like a tv detective just trying to get the story right—he asks and so I tell him. We spend a day in a van looking at locations, I look at buildings that could be the shelter and say, You need a big room for the dorm, a big room for the dining hall, you need doors that lead to staircases, but he already knows all this. I look at the coat (black leather) I will wear, the truck I will drive (beat-up Toyota—production refers to it as the "hero" truck), the woman I will fall in love with (punky, yet kind), I say this one, more than this one, but does this mean it will be any closer to reality, any closer to the truth?

● ● ●

I never went to the police station to retrieve my mother's guns—for all I know, they are still locked in a room somewhere. Or else one day they were auctioned off. Or else they simply vanished. Maybe someone uses one of them every year (the shotgun) to shoot a deer, to feed his family, or maybe someone used another one, the same gun my mother used (the .38), to end his (or her) life. Maybe I should have retrieved them, melted them down, I could have forged them into something—an urn, something big enough to sleep in, *and the world become a bell we'd crawl inside | and the ringing all we'd eat.*

# NINE

**(1986)** I go to Paris for the winter, in part to get away from the shelter, in part to cross paths with Beckett, who I'd read would frequent a certain café every afternoon for a glass of red wine. I'd wander the streets, hoping to run into him, but (surprise) never did. I'd read all the plays, and at Shakespeare and Company I bought a used copy of the trilogy—*Malloy, Malone Dies, The Unnamable.* This is what I remember: a man dragging himself across a field with a spoon, a man ruminating on what he called a *suck stone,* which one should place in one's mouth when hunger or thirst becomes unbearable. Beckett spent a page on how important it was to find the right suck stone—small but not too small, smooth but with character—how to test it in your mouth, for comfort. After that, for years I carried a stone with me wherever I went, in my pocket or in my mouth—it seemed at least as important as a map. That winter in Paris I also scraped together a few francs to see *Oh Les Beaux Jours* (*Happy Days*), a revival with the actress (Madeleine Renaud) who had originated the role in 1961. It opens with a shrieking alarm and blinding lights, to reveal a woman buried up to her waist in sand, yet seemingly unfazed by it. The second act opens with the same alarm and light, only now the woman is buried up to her neck, still unfazed. While in Paris I also tracked down a screening of the one collaboration Beckett did with Buster Keaton, a film called, simply, *Film*—a robed

Keaton, alone in a room, sits in a chair, looks at the closed door, seemingly troubled, or perhaps it's just his face. He hears something at the door—is he hallucinating? He gets up, opens it, a cat rushes in. Keaton throws it out, but it slips back in before he gets the door closed. Repeat. He begins to see eyes everywhere, in the patterns on the back of the chair, on his buttons, in the knots on the door. Everything is looking at him. It would be another year before my father would get himself evicted and end up at the shelter, another year before I'd cease being invisible there.

IT turns out that *Film* doesn't take place entirely in a room—it actually begins outside, under the Brooklyn Bridge (how did I forget a whole bridge?), as Keaton makes his (uncomfortable? paranoid?) way to his room. I thought he was the only actor in the film, but he passes a couple on the street, and a woman on the staircase, and has interactions (of sorts) with each of them. And the cat, I remembered it as a stray, an interloper, but the cat is his, along with a dog (a chihuahua—how could I forget a chihuahua?), a goldfish, and a caged bird. The film begins with a quote on a title card by the Irish philosopher Berkeley—*esse est percipi* (to be is to be perceived), though the actual quote is *esse est percipi aut percipere* (to be is to be perceived and to perceive). Once he makes it into his room, Keaton spends the rest of the film covering whatever it is that seems to be looking at him—that's the part I remember.

**ESSE** *est percipi*. To be is to be perceived. This reminds me of Schrödinger's cat, the thought experiment, you know how it goes—you put a cat put in a box with some sort of a device that may or may not kill him. Without opening the box the question becomes whether the cat is alive or dead (or both alive *and* dead), whether reality is made manifest only when we observe it, whether it is our attention that makes it one thing or another. Is the cat really both alive and dead until the box is opened? Is it possible he is dead in the box, yet alive in some parallel universe? Yet (maybe? obviously?) it isn't just us (humans) who observe the world— maybe (like in *Film*) everything does. If we concede that the cat can observe itself, is this enough to determine its fate? Or maybe the cat is simply dead, at least in this particular box, which is all we have. Accept it, move on.

**WERNER** Heisenberg discovered (invented?) the idea that everything changes in the presence of something else (part of his uncertainty principle), but what is not in the presence of something else? At the very least aren't we always in the presence of time? I'd been working at the shelter for three years before my father got himself evicted and ended up on the streets, but I still get asked if I went to work at the shelter to find him. I don't think this is an unreasonable question. Maybe I went to the shelter to understand men who were very much like my father—marginal, alcoholic, delusional—but it is only one piece of the puzzle. Maybe my father got himself evicted so that we would have a reunion in the shelter, yet I don't know if anyone could have planned such a reunion. My mother had killed herself a year and a half before I started working at the shelter—I felt a need to dissolve myself into something larger than myself, or, I feared, I would follow her. The shelter, it seemed, was larger.

**WHAT** I mean by something larger than myself is changeable—for a while it was the ocean, so I moved onto it, and for the next ten years I lived on a boat, off and on. Before that marijuana had fulfilled the role of something larger than myself, a constant companion, it seemed to connect me to the universe, until it (marijuana? the universe?) began to shrink, until it became a little ocean, until the day came when I'd get high and never leave the boat, never make it to shore, not for days on end. Then poetry, for a while, I'd dream dreams made entirely of words, of sound. Some days it was abandon, some nights it was fucking. Bees for a while, then Abu Ghraib—both perhaps manifestations of a self-righteous anger based on something I read in the newspaper, something I heard on the radio. Thich Nhat Hanh says that the self is made of only non-self elements (*it is the emptiness of the bowl that creates the bowl*). Maurice Halbwachs offers this:

> Often we deem ourselves the originators of thoughts and ideas, feelings and passions, actually inspired by some group. Our agreement with those about us is so complete that we vibrate in unison, ignorant of the real source of the vibrations. How often do we present, as deeply held convictions, thoughts borrowed from a newspaper, book, or conversation? They respond so well to our way of seeing things

that we are surprised to discover that their author is someone other than ourself.

Damasio would seem to dispute, or at least to complicate, this idea
of collective memory: *Consciousness is an entirely private, first-
person phenomenon which occurs as part of a private, first-person
process we call mind.* Yet Damasio goes on to say that attention—
focused attention—is as necessary to consciousness as having
images. When my father appeared at the shelter door he was little
more than an image, two-dimensional, without flesh. I couldn't
know he wouldn't leave, that he wouldn't get off the street, for five
years. I'd been working at the shelter for three years at that point,
I did my job well, or well enough. No one at the shelter asks where
you come from—everyone is there for a reason, yet rarely does the
reason manifest itself. I became, the moment my father walked
through the shelter door, transparent.

Or do I mean real?

**SCHRÖDINGER'S** cat, the uncertainty principle, nonself elements—all of these ideas are in the realm of quantum physics. Reading up on it led me, uneasily, to a term I had yet to encounter: quantum suicide. I have a hard time grasping the concept of quantum suicide, yet it somehow lines up with the concept of quantum immortality, but only if certain parallel universe, many world-worlds interpretations, are true (or even possible). Hugh Everett III, the American physicist who proposed the many-worlds theory, believed that it guaranteed him immortality—he argued that consciousness is bound at each branching to follow whichever path does not lead to death. In this way the cat is both alive and dead. Or, better yet, it lives forever. But does this desire (can desire?) change the way it is?

**DISSOLVE** into something larger. I never utter the word *God*, even when I pray (which I almost never do, being a devout nonbeliever). I believe that anything I can name, anything I can understand, cannot possibly help me, not with this. What is this? Everything. As Whitman offered: *Dazzling and tremendous how quick the sunrise would kill me, if I could not now and always send sun-rise out of me.* Once I said God is everything that is not me, but today I'm not so sure. Thoreau distills it all down to this: Only that day dawns to which we are awake.

# TEN

**(2011)** One day, in early January, the money starts to flow—the film is *green-lit*, which makes it real. Apparently it hadn't been real until this moment—everyone (apparently) had been going on faith. The lunches weren't real, the script wasn't real, Hollywood wasn't real. De Niro wasn't real, Julianne wasn't real—it all could have collapsed at any moment. Now, with the money flowing, it is closer to real. I get several calls a day now, mostly from Paul. Today he is at the dentist's—De Niro is having some teeth pulled, to get ready for the part. *Teeth?* A couple years ago, apparently, De Niro needed some implants, and knowing he was going to, or might, play a homeless man, he had temporary teeth put in—placeholders—and now he is having them removed. In one scene in his descent he will get beaten, robbed—*rolled* is the word we use when a drunk gets robbed. He is having some teeth removed so he can (I imagine) embody damage. Paul puts De Niro on the phone.

How's your father's teeth? he asks.

**PAUL** Dano will play me, not as a boy but as an adult, a younger version of the me I have become. At twenty-seven he's the age I was when my father first appeared at the shelter. I'd thought it was important that the actors playing us be approximately the ages we were—at the time I was in my late twenties and my father was in his late fifties. My father was thirty when I was born, still thirty when he left us, or we left him (it's still unclear who left whom). In the film my father has to contain the potential to pull out of his tailspin, and fulfill his vision of himself as "America's greatest living writer." He cannot be pitiable. We must believe, on some level, his claim that he is above the situation he finds himself in—he has to embody a degree of both grandeur and menace, which is why De Niro is perfect for the part. At the time I believed that my father could destroy me, if I allowed him in too deeply. Does this mean Dano has to believe that he could be destroyed? I am speaking here only of myself; when one has not yet made it out of one's twenties, one has to feign an air of solidity, when it isn't yet deeply felt. One is still so unsure, one has to be careful, all the time, watching where one's feet fall. It's tiring, this endless uncertainty, which is perhaps why I would so easily burst into moments of such senseless self-destruction. By the time I made it to my mid-thirties my father had lost some of his bite, he'd become someone who genuinely needed my help or else he would go under (we will all go under one day, I know, but we don't have to die out on the streets). By the time I was thirty-five I was able to offer him my hand at times, but when I was still in my twenties my father could destroy me, at least this was how it appeared.

**EASTER** is known as the time of "bright sadness." *Lent* means, simply, "spring"—from the Germanic word for "long," since the days, in springtime, are visibly longer. From Lent till Easter, these are the days we'll be filming. In the latest version of the script, after I first meet my father (after he is evicted), I tell the woman I am sleeping with that I don't know if I ever want to see him again. I suggest to Paul that we cut that line in the script, but Paul says we can't: *You have to deny your father three times, like Peter—it's part of the structure of the whole.* Peter, you remember, was told that he would deny Jesus three times before the cock crowed, but he did not believe it. Yet in some parallel (biblical) universe, it had already happened—preordained, written, inevitable. *The second time you deny your father,* Paul tells me, *is when you tell another worker, "That guy has nothing to do with me, he's just a drunk and a con man." The third time is when he comes up for barring, and you simply watch the other hands go up.*

The rooster crows. I never noticed.

I get a call to be in Tribeca at noon (De Niro's office)—today is the day of the table read, where a dozen actors, each with a role or two, will read the script out loud, to see how the words feel in their mouths (I guess). Coffee and bagels, we shake hands all around, each will pretend to be someone I once knew. We sit. De Niro opens his mouth and my father comes out, then Dano opens his mouth and I come out, then Julianne opens her mouth. De Niro pretends, Dano pretends, Julianne pretends. Day of the dead, dawn of the dead, I sit off to one side, pretending to watch myself, pretending I'm here, but I'm not, not really. My disembodied family, risen from the grave, sitting around a table, laughing. Fucken tower of babel, I'm nearly erased. Sometimes they speak their own words, sometimes the words I wrote, sometimes the words Paul wrote. The walls around us thrum with posters of De Niro— mohawked De Niro, head-bandaged De Niro, boxer De Niro. Then my mother pretends to throw herself in the ocean again, then my father pretends to sleep outside again, then my girlfriend pretends to break up with me again, then we pretend to make love. I'm here, watching us make love, pretending to understand, pretending to have forgiven everything, to have been forgiven.

**A** question—*What am I doing here?*—passes through me whenever someone closes his mouth, whenever the words stop. A production office has been set up across town, on the west side near the Film Forum, I've heard about it but I've yet to see it. We are now in a state of *preproduction*—no camera rolling, no call sheets, not yet. Now is the time of questions, time to line the physics of the world up with my memory of that world. Why is it important for Julianne to know what my mother's hair was like, for De Niro to know what jacket my father would wear? What does it matter if my father carried a flask or drank straight from the bottle? Later she will cut her hair, and he will put on the right jacket, and they will appear. Now she merely opens her mouth, says the words—*He'll show up*—then De Niro opens his mouth, says the words—*The question is why she stuck around as long as she did*. This imitation of life, this simulacrum, this déjà vu—this is what was said (is this what is said?)—will these actors, these strangers, replace my family? Will they move in, somehow, push their way inside me, so that soon I won't have to tell them a thing? Imitation, according to Plato, distracted people from reality, from the truth. Mimesis, to use Plato's word, creates an alternate reality—through a play, say—which will draw us away, distract us, from the truth of this life. Yet mimesis, it would

136

seem, can only come from close attention to the world, and this close attention (as Weil points out) is a type of prayer, another (possible) way to escape the cage of ego. To dissolve into something larger.

*IT is the emptiness of the bowl that creates the bowl.* I meet Paul at his hotel to help him decide between two actors who are being considered to play me as an eleven-year-old. Paul sets me up with his computer to watch clips of each. One, reading a letter my father has sent from prison (*My writing is going very—very—well*), stumbles a little on his lines—one could believe that at that moment he is just learning how to read. The other is more polished—cuter, in a way, but it seems he knows he's cuter. His voice is higher, which at first marks him as innocent, but at some point I sense that he is already getting high, that he has already gotten laid—something in his eyes is a bit too knowing, and something in me needs him to be innocent. I tell Paul this, and he agrees. We go with the innocent.

I tell a friend in Texas that the film is green-lit, that I will likely be on set every day, and she sends me a copy of *My Winnipeg*, Guy Maddin's book based on his film. It might help you, she says, in case you decide to write about it. *My Winnipeg* is the opposite, or perhaps the mirror, of Kiarostami's *Close-Up*. Where Kiarostami used real people to reenact a moment from their lives, Maddin hires a group of actors to return to his childhood home and act out certain memories of his childhood. Where Maddin lines up with Kiarostami is by hiring his mother (who may or may not have been an actress in her youth) to play his mother. In one scene she has trouble remembering her lines, even though she was, presumably, the one who said them the first time around. Our film will not be a documentary, any more than *My Winnipeg*, or *Close-Up*. It isn't my life, Paul Dano isn't me. In the script the last scene has Dano giving a reading from his first book of poems—we will use my book (*Some Ether*) as a prop. De Niro will show up to listen, I will pick the poem Dano will read. My father never came to hear me read my poems, I never invited him. In this scene Dano will sit in a chair and read, *If you find yourself lost, dig a cave in the snow, quickly*. . . . (I never realized that poem was about my father until I heard Dano read it.) At the end of this scene (which will be the end of the film), I will introduce my father to my wife and child (which I have done), and I will let my father hold his granddaughter (which he has done). The film will suggest that I figured out how to write a book and become a father in a couple years—in reality it will take ten years for the book to come out, and ten more years for Maeve to appear.

# ELEVEN

**IN** Beckett's *Krapp's Last Tape*, the eponymous main character spends the tail end of his birthday interacting with his former self. He does this by listening to an audiotape he made thirty years ago, on his thirty-ninth birthday. Making this tape is, or was (apparently), a ritual of sorts, a summing up of the year he'd just lived. It is unclear if the "last" in the title means that the last tape he made is the one he is listening to, or if the last tape is the one he is making tonight, as in the final tape, no more after this one. Krapp searches for a specific spool as a memory flitters across his mind, as a thought occurs to him, as he remembers a moment, a year. He finds the tape, forwards through it until he gets to the part he is looking for—this moment is, at times, bittersweet. (Once wasn't enough for you. [*Pause.*] Lie down across her.) A man alone in a room at the end of his life. It's hard to rewind your memory to the exact spot that once gave you comfort.

**FOR** a while after my mother died, a few years, I kept a postcard near me—a stop-motion photograph of a bullet caught midflight, just after having pierced an apple. I would find the postcard in a book I was reading, or it would fall out of the notebook I was writing in. The photograph of the bullet piercing the apple is from a series of stop-motion photographs—a drop of milk making a white crown in a glass, a match head as it ignites. As might be expected, the entry hole into the apple is clean, but the exit wound has blown the skin all to shit. This apple is my mother, I'd think, holding her in my hands. The bullet hangs not an inch from the apple—it looks like it could either go on forever or simply drop to the ground with a small clatter.

●  ●  ●

**REBECCA** Solnit offers this:

> In the spring of 1872 a man photographed a horse. The resulting photograph does not survive, but from this first encounter of a camera-bearing man with a fast-moving horse sprang a series of increasingly successful experiments that produced thousands of extant images. The photographs are well known, but they are most significant as the bridge to a new art that would transform the world. By the end of the 1870s, these experiments had led to the photographer's invention of the essentials of motion-picture technology. He had captured aspects of motion whose speed had made them as invisible as the moons of Jupiter before the telescope, and he had found a way to set them back in motion. It was as though he had grasped time itself, made it stand still, and then made it run again, over and over. Time was at his command as it had never been at anyone's before.

*As though he had grasped time itself....* Film, we know, does nothing to time itself, merely to our perception of it—we can speed it up, slow it down, rearrange it, stop it anywhere we choose. Film makes time appear to repeat, but nothing repeats, nothing comes back, nothing returns, except the feeling of what returns. In

Buster Keaton's *The Cameraman* (1928), the character Keaton plays falls in love with a woman who works in the newsreel department of MGM, so he decides to become a news photographer. Yet when he screens his first attempts we see that he has created a mishmash of double exposures—a battleship is now anchored on Broadway, cars drive into other cars and right through them, a diver enters a swimming pool and then rises back out of the water and back onto the board. He leaves the screening as a failure, yet in some ways this seems closer to reality, or at least to how we experience it, than the lie that time is unspooling chronologically.

I walked out of the shelter one day, the shelter where I'd worked for nearly seven years, and didn't cross the threshold again for nearly ten years. I didn't exactly quit—I just never went back. In the film I will shake hands with my coworkers, say goodbye, but this was not how it happened. My father was still living on the streets when I left, still a guest at the inn, when he wasn't barred from it. I decided to go back after I'd been working on the book for nearly five years, after I'd gone as far as I could into my memory of the shelter. I wanted to read over the logs we'd kept, the notes I'd written, in order to find the page where my father first appeared at the door, and the page, a couple years later, when we voted to bar him. This barring scene will appear in the film—in the film it will be the third time I deny my father (the rooster crows). In life I denied my father over and over. In life (and in the film), when it is time to vote I will not raise my hand, not to bar him, nor to allow him to stay. I will sit empty-eyed and let it happen.

**(1999)** I call Pine Street and ask to be connected with someone in administration. I explain that I'm working on a book about my years working there, and that I'm hoping to read the logs from that time. The woman I'm speaking with connects me with Lyndia (the director)—that we know each other helps, it means I don't need to explain why I'm doing what I'm doing, why I need to see the logs. I don't know if I could have told her why, even if she'd asked. Lyndia, it turns out, had married a former guest: You remember Mike _____. (I don't remember.) She promises to try to locate the logs, but warns that it might be hard.

**AT** some point the logs had been boxed and shipped to Long Island Shelter, stored and forgotten in a damp basement. Lyndia sent a worker in a van to retrieve them, all ten boxes. On the day of my appointment, on my way to Pine Street from South Station (I'd taken the train up from New York), I stop into J.J. Foley's, a bar I hadn't set foot into for over ten years. I'd quit drinking when I was still working at the shelter, just before I began working on the Van. Before that Foley's had been the bar I'd spent most of my off-duty time in—I can say I loved Foley's as much as I loved any place on this earth. When I walk back in, Jimmy the bartender (maybe he's the owner as well?) is where I'd left him ten long years ago— behind the bar, yet now looking (understandably) older, maybe even a-few-teeth-missing older. Paler. It's ten in the morning. I stand in front of Jimmy until he looks up. Not missing a beat, he smiles: Nick, haven't seen you around for a while, how you been? It's been ten years, I say. Then he reaches into the well and puts a Harp on the bar.

**LAMAR** could be found every night in a parking garage near J.J. Foley's. He would take whatever we offered—sandwiches, coffee, blankets—but he would never come in. His clothes were always filthy, his pants often torn. He'd ask for a new pair, and I'd ask him what size, and he'd say thirty-eight. I'd tell him I'd be back on the Van Sunday night, and he'd say, Sunday? What's the date Sunday? Twenty-first, I'd say, and he'd smile. Twenty-first is too late— world's ending on the twentieth. When I was working with the homeless I sometimes felt, though I didn't often articulate it, that a bomb had been dropped on Boston and we were all simply wandering through the wreckage. After politely refusing Jimmy's ten a.m. Harp, as I make my way to Pine Street, I stop at Lamar's garage—amazing and strange that this beat-up concrete box is still standing. But, of course, Lamar is nowhere to be found— even then he was almost never here.

THE guy working the front door at Pine Street doesn't even glance at my face as I raise my arms for the frisk. I tell the girl working the front desk (army boots, vintage dress, tattoos—I'd have dogged her if it was still then) that I'm here to see Lyndia. The guy who frisked me hears me ask for Lyndia, comes over, apologizes. It's fine, I tell him, if you hadn't frisked me I'd have been upset. To imagine I wasn't scruffy anymore, to imagine I'd changed that much. He directs me upstairs, points to a door—I know the staircase, it leads to the showers. As I climb, another doorway appears, off to the right—they'd done some renovations since I'd last been inside. Lyndia appears at this door, we embrace, she leads me through a suite of offices, which also hadn't been there, or if they had I'd never gone up into them. When I worked here, in my twenties, I wore sweaters lifted from the clothing room, I did a lot of drugs. I didn't belong upstairs, in administration. I belonged on the floor, with the guys.

**TEN** boxes of logs await me, stacked in the corner of the conference room. Each log is simply a three-ring black vinyl binder, each holding a hundred white-lined pages. My own Dead Sea Scrolls—some have water damage, some already unreadable. We got to them just in time, Lyndia tells me. She gives me the code to the copy machine, points to a huge conference table I can spread out on, then she leaves me alone. I open the first box, pull out the topmost binder, look on the first page for the date. I want 1984, the year I started, I want to see what I wrote. I want 1987, the year my father was evicted. I want the entry that first named him—new guest—appearing at the door. I want 1989, which I think was the year we barred him, for being out of control. The logs smell like I remember—musty nicotine, panicky sweat. I spent that first day randomly opening pages, looking for my handwriting, but more often than not I'd simply get lost in a thread of thought. I went back every day for a week, it was like watching a movie, only the speed was off, as one image, one event, one disaster, folded into the next, and then the next. A name rose up—Black Cat Sam, say—then twenty pages later, or maybe it was five binders later, Black Cat was dead, dropped off by the police one night, left outside on a bench, likely already dead when they picked him up. I'd forgotten about Black Cat—

what was gained by reliving his death, I cannot say. But I'm glad he came back, glad for the time before he was dead, when I got to write the note about him checking into detox, glad for the chance to remember how hopeful that made us.

# TWELVE

I send a note to Paul Dano, offering to meet up. I get a note back: Sure, that'd be great. I assume he's read the script by now, but I don't know if he's read the book, so I go to my local bookstore to buy him a copy. The owner (Zack) is a pal, I ask him if they have any in stock. As he checks the computer I tell him about the impending movie, he says he's already heard—Dano was in a couple days ago, he lives around the corner. As he says this I see my book on the reserved shelf behind him. Zack picks it up, glances at the slip of paper tucked inside it, smiles—Dano's name is on the slip, apparently he'd ordered it when he came in. Strange to see his name in my book. Should I sign it to him? I ask. Sure, Zack says. I hold the book open, the pen balanced over the title page. I don't know Paul Dano. I write, *I am you as you are me....*

I don't know if this is true or merely (merely?) apocryphal, but another actor, a younger actor (not Dano), was supposed to play the preacher in *There Will Be Blood*. But the younger actor freaked out at the way Daniel Day-Lewis (an actor who, I hear, immerses himself completely in whatever character he plays) would glare at him day in, day out, on set and off. During lunch. In the makeup trailer. In video village. Day-Lewis, whose character declares at one point, *I just don't like people*, glared at everyone. It didn't bother Dano, and so he became the preacher—the preacher who baptizes a reluctant Day-Lewis, the preacher Day-Lewis bludgeons to death at the end.

**DANO** and I meet a few days later at a local restaurant. He orders a meatloaf sandwich, I order the same. I never order meatloaf, I don't know why I do this—shouldn't he order what I order? He tells me he's halfway through the book, that he likes it. I tell him I like his work as well. We sit at a table facing each other, get right into it. He already knows a bit about me from the book. He tells me something about himself—his upbringing, his parents' divorce, his mother's struggles. I don't need to know all this, but it helps, somehow. He grew up in New York, I'm looking closely at his face as he speaks. What am I looking for? It's like looking into a mirror and seeing nothing, it's like drawing a self-portrait and finding you have no idea what you look like. He asks if I always dress up when I give a reading. What? He saw a clip of me giving a reading on YouTube, in it I'm wearing a suit jacket. No, I tell him, that was unusual. Any rituals, he asks, before you get up on stage? I think for a moment. I just need to be in my body, I tell him, but I've yet to find one surefire way to do that. I look at my coffee. If I drink coffee my consciousness ends up slightly outside my body, I tell him, so that I end up watching myself as I read—this consciousness is always judgmental, always murmuring, *This isn't going very well, you're losing them. . . .*

**BY** Christmas we are a family. We have a mother, one who had a lot of different boyfriends, who may or may not have been an addict. We have a son, one who wandered the saltmarshes alone as a child (do I tell Dano this?), one who is definitely an addict. We have a father, one who drove a taxi off and on his whole life, who robbed banks (without a gun), landing in federal prison for three-to-five. A father who may or may not have been tortured in federal prison, who ends up sleeping on the streets for a few years. A father who, once he started (he claims he didn't start drinking until he was twenty), drank a bottle of vodka every day of his life, except (maybe) when he was broke, or in prison, where he was likely drugged (he was held in the medical wings). Who is, perhaps, the one person I can point to as the reason I no longer drink (or smoke marijuana), if there is, or needs to be, a reason. Yet I could just as easily point to him as the reason I sought oblivion, though this would not be true. My family, it seems, has been seeking oblivion forever.

●　●　○

A few days before we start filming, Dano sends me an email:

Did you ever:

Wear an earring? (I can picture one on my Nick, unsure if necessary)

A necklace?

Rings?

A chain wallet?

Have some sort of key chain for work/home?

Did you carry a flask? (I was curious if it could be good for the van segment where he is hitting rock bottom to carry a flask . . .)

Do you have any tattoos?

Did you wear a watch?

Where are your scars?

# THIRTEEN

**A** man holds up an axe, says, This axe belonged to my grandfather—the head has been replaced three times, and the handle has been replaced four times. You might note—rightly—that the grandfather's hand never touched this axe, and yet the man still believes it is the same axe he wielded. In Japan there is a temple said to be four thousand years old. When you visit you will read that it burned to the ground over a thousand years ago, yet it was rebuilt exactly the same—exact same design, exact same materials, yet the important detail is that the replica results from the same idea—the same *intention*—as the original. This is what makes the temple the same.

**(2007)** In the years waiting for the movie to get made, my father's condition worsened. *A man alone in a room at the end of his life.* Since he got off the streets he continued to pour at least a fifth of vodka into his body daily, at least until his disability check ran out—really, there was only one way his condition could go, and that was down. Now, once again, he is on the brink of eviction (his hoarding's a fire hazard, he's threatened a child, he's stopped paying his rent, whatever), and there is nowhere that will take him in, besides a shelter. The other option is for me to take him in, which isn't really an option. In a desperate attempt to keep him from ending up back on the streets, I contact a doctor I know from my time working at the shelter (Jim O'Connell), who sets up a physical—to qualify for any assistance my father needs to be evaluated. His tests reveal that at some point in the previous months he'd suffered a minor stroke, which partially explains his deepening deterioration. He is sent to a hospital for another evaluation, and from there to a rehab, and from there to a long-term care facility—Roscommon, like the county in Ireland.

● ● ●

**ROSCOMMON**—every time I visit I need to ask someone at the front desk for the code, so I can take the elevator up the one flight (or is it two?) to his room. The elevators, as well as the doors to the outside, can only be opened if you know the code (in this way it resembles a film set). On my second visit I get off on the wrong floor—for some reason all the rooms on this floor are being broken down, emptied. The metal bedframes disassembled, the phones at the front desk gone, their wires connected to nothing now. It's a ghost floor, eerie, as if everyone on it had died at once. I go to where my father's room should be, past all the other empty rooms, just in case he is the only one left, but that room is, of course, also empty. Back at the elevator I forget the code to get back on, so I wander the empty hallways, find a door with a window in it, a window reinforced with steel mesh, and beyond that window I see nurses and orderlies and old people in wheelchairs going in and out of rooms. That hallway is lit, the hallway I'm in is dark. This door cannot be opened (of course) without the code, so I knock on the window to get an orderly's attention. She comes to the window, I mouth, wide-eyed, *Please open the door.*

*You need the code,* she mouths back, and points in the direction of the keypad.

*I'm not a resident*, I mouth.

The orderly shakes her head, turns her back, goes on with her mopping.

**WHEN** does a thing stop being itself? At one point in the film De Niro will taunt Dano (as my father taunted me), insisting, You are me, I made you. Dano will shout back, I am not you. When the film is done I will show this scene to my father and he will perk up, and even begin imitating De Niro's imitation of him: Listen to his voice, *You are me*—his voice is great. In the paradox of the grandfather's axe, some relativist interpreters of Buddhism would say, elliptically, that it can be said to be your grandfather's axe until it ceases to function as your grandfather's axe. Another strand of Buddhism might say that it was never your grandfather's axe at all—the self is made up only of nonself elements. My father, before his eviction, before we relocated him to Roscommon, would, at times, brandish a spiked club inches from my face. He would, at times, threaten to take out my jugular (*Someday, son, this awl will be yours*). At these moments I'd simply stare him down, I'd learned to do that (*like a tree learns to swallow barbed wire*). This was the club he'd carry for protection, the years he drove a cab in Boston. When Paul visited him for the first time, my father held this same club inches from his head—Paul didn't flinch. When I moved my father to Roscommon I put the club in a box in my attic. De Niro wants to see it, to hold it. I bring it to his office, pass it to him—it looks small in his hand. It's decided that the props guy will make a bigger one, one that will read as more threatening, mythic—one De Niro can *wield*.

**THE** paradox of the grandfather's axe is a version of the Ship of Theseus, the question of whether a ship whose wood is completely replaced remains the same ship. This paradox has been wrestled with by Heraclitus, Socrates, Plato, Plutarch: When does a thing stop being itself? When does a person? In *The Wonderful Wizard of Oz* (the book, 1900), a lumberjack has an axe that is cursed—one by one it chops off all his limbs, which are replaced by tin replicas, until finally even the torso and head are replaced and he becomes the Tin Woodsman.

Two years into my father's homeless odyssey he claimed his toes needed to be amputated—he'd been sleeping out too many snowy nights. When I was eighteen I traded my spleen for a bottle of peppermint schnapps and a midnight motorcycle ride. You could say that the bottle functioned, for my father, and then for me, as an axe. In real life, afterward, you simply hobble on—no one replaces the missing toes, or the broken spleen.

# FOURTEEN

**A** ziplock plastic bag full of Homies is on the conference table in the recently rented production office. Homies are small action figures that come in bubblegum machines and cost fifty cents each. Paul uses one for each character to storyboard our movie, he pushes them around on a table to show the cinematographer where he imagines each actor will be in each shot. My father looks like Johnny Cash—black cowboy hat, long black coat. I look like a wide-eyed urchin—shirtless, suspenders, carrying a banjo.

**THE** costume designer (Aude) comes into De Niro's office with a collection of bags. We need to pick two—one for when my father first appears at the shelter, one for when he's been out on the streets awhile. When my father crossed the threshold he was still holding his life together, or trying to appear to be holding it together. For that we decide on a red and blue Naugahyde flight bag—stylish, in a downtrodden way. The other one, the one he will carry after he is barred from the shelter and living on the streets, is, simply, a paper bag with some duct tape holding it together. I point out that there should be more tape around the handles in the final scenes, that the paper bag should be inside a plastic bag, to keep it from the weather. De Niro and Aude refer to my father as Jonathan: This is for when Jonathan has been sleeping outside for a few months, she says.

**SEVEN** of us pile into a van to visit abandoned Catholic schools as possible locations for Pine Street. Several of these schools have been recently closed down—the Catholic Church has hit hard times, between the sex scandals and the economy. We visit four or five—each looks perfect, each still thick with an air of punitive charity. The one we settle on—St. Patrick's—is in Little Italy. In one room, on a bulletin board, the word INSPIRE is written out in two-foot-high letters, using clear pushpins, though it has been left unfinished. In another room *Martin Scorsese went to this school* is chalked onto a blackboard. Paul asks if it could pass for the shelter, and I look around: If we line up enough beds in the gym, sure. Almost anywhere could be a shelter—people sleep in trashbags and in cardboard boxes. If there is nowhere else they sleep where they fall.

**WHEN** he was shipped to Roscommon I salvaged several boxes of my father's things—notebooks, manuscripts, photographs, books, letters, ephemera. It's all in the attic of a house my pal Debra lives in upstate. At my request she culls it down to one box to send to De Niro—on top she places a letter where my father concedes that I might win a Nobel Prize before him. A few days later I open the box in De Niro's Tribeca office. I pass De Niro a photograph of my father as a young man, wearing a tie and a plaid vest and a suitcoat, posing in front of what looks like a grounded fishing trawler. He's good-looking, De Niro says. Everything he wears is a costume, I tell him. A rubber band holds several small notebooks together, the top one has *Montag's Blue Horse Notebook* on the cover, a horse's head centered between the words. The writing inside is in my father's handwriting—light pencil, hard to decipher. At the bottom of one box are four worn orange binders—my father's unpublished novel, *The Button Man*. I pass them to De Niro. *The Button Man* is the project my father put all his chips into, what he gambled his whole life on.

**PAUL** looks through the boxes for one letter—the rejection from Viking Press, which describes my father's writing as *a virtuoso display of personality (yet its dosage would kill hardier readers than we have here)*. Paul imagines my father—De Niro—carrying this letter with him everywhere as a totemic object, unfolding it when his faith in himself flags. After *Suck City* came out, a woman got in touch with me—she'd written another rejection letter to my father, this one from Little, Brown. She told me that she sincerely admired his writing, yet she was only an assistant, she wasn't the one who made the decision about who to publish. The name she signed to all her rejection letters (Sandra Brown) was not her own—a pseudonym to protect her from disgruntled writers. My father had Sandra Brown subpoenaed to testify as to his character and talent when he was being sentenced for robbing banks—this was how he discovered that Sandra Brown did not exist. Telling the story now, he still seems genuinely crushed, more crushed about that than about the part where he's sentenced, which he relates with what seems like bravado. In the boxes Debra sent us I find a letter that suggests that the woman he knew as Sandra Brown eventually ended up knowing my father a little better than as simply another rejected writer.

● ● ●

**AUDE** sends me a link to photographs of De Niro dressed in various outfits. I'm unsure what I'm supposed to say—this one with the sweater looks like something my father would wear, but this one with the trenchcoat looks like someone who is trying to pass himself off as a dandy, which is something my father would do. A light-colored coat or a dark-colored coat? Scully cap? Fedora? And how will it change over the course of the film? What will he lose, what will he replace it with? We are trying to contain seven years into one hundred minutes, we will have seven weeks to do this, we've been working on it for seven years. Aude tells me that it is eerie, the parallels between her father and my father, that she will tell me the story one day.

• • •

**A** producer (Andrew) is on the phone with a lawyer for Focus, they are asking me about characters in the book, they need to know if anyone will sue us. Beady-Eyed Bill? Alice? Marie? Skid? All homeless, all were living on the extreme margins of the city, it is unlikely any are still alive. Your father? I can sign for my father. Ivan? Richard? Both dead.

Good, the lawyer says.

# FIFTEEN

**ON** *Radiolab* I hear a story about a long-term care facility in Germany that has a problem—a resident will sometimes make it through the doors to the outside and wander off. It can take hours, or days, to find him, and in those hours, those days, terrible things can happen. The facility strikes upon a possible solution—they will set up a fake bus stop outside the building, on the sidewalk where a bus stop might be. It will be, essentially, a stage set. The plan works—now, when a patient escapes, she goes straight to the bus stop and waits, until a nurse or an orderly comes out, sits beside her. If this were a play, this is how it would begin. It's a beautiful day, the orderly says, where are you going? No matter what the resident answers, the orderly says, O, I'm going there as well. They talk awhile, waiting for a bus that will never come. Then, when the resident forgets what it is she is waiting for, the orderly asks if she'd like to have lunch, and they go back inside. Of course, the facility has to explain to the rest of the neighborhood that no bus will ever pull up to that stop.

**THE** first time I visit my father in Roscommon he's a wreck, barely lucid, seemingly overmedicated. Drugs are necessary, a nurse tells me, to detox him. It seems he won't last much longer. The next time I visit, a couple months later, he's transformed—his hair is cut, combed, he's gained back a little weight. Pleasure to see you, he says, like he always says. He is, I realize, not drunk. This is the first time I have ever seen my father not drunk—is this his true self? They treat me like I'm a millionaire here, he tells me. Three meals a day, doctors, a room, but I got no money. I don't know who's paying for all this. Don't worry, I tell him, we'll work it out, you just get better. The next time I visit he takes me aside, asks if I can give him a lift to Scituate, he wants to visit his father—his father died forty years ago, I see no need to tell him this. He can crash with his old friend Ronnie Fallon—*Rotten Ronnie*. He lives up on Third Cliff, my father tells me. I know, I say—I think Ronnie is dead as well, but I'm not sure. I say, Sure, we'll go to Scituate next time. When I visit next I'll bring him a painting of Scituate that had hung on his apartment wall. I'll bring him a potted plant, a leafy thing (he'd had many plants in his last apartment). I'll bring him a copy of my book. The next time I visit all these things will be gone.

**IN** a play or a film, when one is supposed to be drunk, a bad actor will stumble and slur. A good actor will hold himself more upright, speak even more clearly, more precisely, and only if you listen closely will you sense the booze seeping out between the words (basic Stanislavsky). *Profound inebriation has stylized their movements so they are invariably too slow, too intricate, too careful, too distracted, or too unpredictable. . . .* I read this in *Artforum*, in a review of Gillian Wearing's *Drunk*. The article describes, in part, the genesis of the piece: the door to Wearing's studio, in London (I think it was London), opened onto the sidewalk, where a group of homeless street alcoholics gathered every day, all day, and drank. One day, Wearing invited the men into her studio, where inside she'd set up a camera, along with several bottles of booze— mostly cheap wine, the same rotgut she'd seen them drinking. Over the next several days, inside her studio, against a white paper backdrop, she filmed them drinking. And falling. And pissing against the backdrop. And stumbling into each other. And trying to hold themselves upright, with dignity. And fighting. And teetering out of the frame.

**DE** Niro will have to drink throughout the film, more often than not from a pint of some nameless rotgut vodka. This is who my father was, this is how he spent his days—he poured vodka into himself. Occasionally he went over the edge—pissing himself, threatening children, wreaking havoc—but more often than not he held it together. He had what we drunks refer to, with pride, as *tolerance*. De Niro asks, What did your father drink? With ice? In a glass? With orange juice? Always with orange juice? Ever from a flask? Straight from the bottle? A pint? A fifth? A quart?

● ● ●

**ANOTHER** version of the paradox of the grandfather's axe is Sorites Paradox, also known as the paradox of the heap (*Grain upon grain, one by one, and one day, suddenly, there's a heap, a little heap, the impossible heap*). It goes like this: Consider a heap of sand, from which grains are removed, one by one. When does it stop being called a heap? Is it still a heap when one grain remains? If not, when did it change from heap to nonheap? A guy who worked at Pine Street when I started—Eddie—used to try to get me to quit drinking. He'd go to his meetings and invite me along. I liked Eddie, but I'd just shake my head—I wasn't like him, I wasn't one of them. When my father stumbled through the door, Eddie again offered his hand, but I still wasn't ready to throw in the towel. Grain upon grain. Eddie had been a stickup man, had done some hard time, and ended up on the streets—almost beat for beat my father's story. To look at him then it was hard to believe he was the same person—at that point he was nearly made of light. He'd distilled his life down to a single room, his work at Pine Street, and meetings—it's hard to remember how much I resented that he could see through me.

**WHEN** I first read about Wearing's piece in *Artforum*, it sounded like little more than voyeurism, a tourist witnessing (is that the right word? provoking?) the suffering of others. I took myself to the gallery, and as I stood before it, as the film loop played, *Drunk* slowly, uncomfortably, convinced me. I can't say why—maybe it's the same reason I went to work with the homeless, or one of the reasons—I was a drunk, maybe not as bad as the street guys, not yet, but drifting close. Part of me knew that I needed to place myself that close to drunks, that close to my (possible) future, if I was to have any chance of pulling out of whatever tailspin I was in. Yet even that didn't work, until my father showed up, and even then it would take two more years for me to even attempt to get sober. Grain upon grain. The drunks in Wearing's piece know they are being filmed—they pose, they mug, they leer—and then they forget.

• • •

ON the wall of the day room of Roscommon is a sign (the words in capital letters are on little signs that velcro to the background sign):

Today is SATURDAY

AUGUST 20 2011

The Season is

SUMMER

The Weather is

HOT and [a drawing of clouds]

The Next Holiday is

LABOR DAY

In *Memory Disorders in Clinical Practice,* Narinder Kapur explains that chronic alcohol consumption can lead to marked memory loss and generalized cognitive defects, as well as "disorientation for time and also place." Forrest Gander offers this: *Certain diseases—such as alcoholism—...tend to devour memories in reverse order to their acquisition.*

# SIXTEEN

**(2009)** If anything happens to my father while he is in Roscommon I get a phone call. He cuts his finger, he falls out of bed, his meds need to be adjusted, I get a call. Do what you have to do to make him comfortable, is all I can think to say. After two years of relative stability he begins, for no apparent reason, to (literally) suffocate—something wrong with his lungs, he's *aspirating*, that's the word the doctor uses. He is taken to a hospital, stabilized, then a few days later he's back at Roscommon, but now he's having difficulty swallowing. After a few weeks they want to ship him back to the hospital, intubate him, hook him up to machines—they need my okay. A week later I send this note to my half-sister, Anastacia:

I just thought of you, and thought to update you on Jonathan.

Did you know he'd moved into a long-term care facility almost two years ago now? His health was slipping, he was no longer able to care for himself, and he landed, as per usual, in a pretty decent situation, considering—Roscommon, in West Roxbury. I see him there every few months, when I can make it to Boston.

He ended up in the hospital a couple months ago, with pneumonia, and I got a flurry of calls from doctors, as to what level of treatment he would want, as he had slipped further into a form of dementia, so was unable to make his own decisions.

After much research, soul searching, and (some) torment, I decided to sign a DNR (do not resuscitate), which means that they will not do major medical intervention on him such as breathing machines, feeding tubes, etc. If his heart stops, they will try to get it started. If he needs medicine, they will give it to him. But nothing beyond that.

That said, I don't know how much longer he will live. He's back in Roscommon, back in the routine he was in before the pneumonia, and seems to be well cared for. He has nurses, physical therapist, aides, and, now, hospice workers. A priest visits him daily. I am going to try to see him tomorrow.

I thought I'd let you know. I hope all's well with you.

Anastacia (known as Stacey) is my half-sister, from my father's second marriage, which ended much like his first (to my mother), with her mother either leaving or throwing him out. Anastacia and I never met, until *Suck City* came out, then she tracked me down, sent a note. At some point I reintroduced her to our father—we met at a diner around the corner from his apartment, ordered eggs, listened to him tell his stories. He and Anastacia had never really met, not since she was an infant, yet he didn't seem particularly interested in her, in what she had made of her life—he already knew she was a ski instructor at Vail, he'd told me as much a hundred times over the years, with a type of pride. What else did he need to know? My father named her Anastacia after the missing czarina, as I am named after the former czar—some days he claims to be a descendant of the Romanovs, though not so much anymore.

● ● ●

IN medieval times monks spent their days, their lives, transcribing the Bible into illuminated manuscripts. Initially some of these texts were written without punctuation—commas, dashes, ellipses—none of it had yet been invented, or if it had it was lost. Suppressed. Not only was there no punctuation, at times there was not even any space between the words, the result being a solid block of text, often framed by illustrations—dragons, antelopes, angels. You've seen these books, we call them *illuminated*. Beautiful, yet the text—no white space, no hesitation, no delay—it was as if they'd forgotten poetry. This was deliberate, arising from what is known as *horror vacui*—the fear of empty space. The fear was—is—that the Devil will flow into any empty space, which is essentially the fear of thought, or of meditation, or of simply allowing the mind to wander. When I think about where my mind wanders, the bad neighborhoods I find myself in, again and again (*I dream only of the orifices of the body, beyond the body is nothing*), perhaps this fear is justified, perhaps I—or my mind—should be kept in a cage. One monk—a rebel, a freethinker—eventually began putting a small mark beside certain words he felt needed emphasis, or that one should linger over for a moment. This opened the door—another monk saw these marks, came up with his own marks, and his own reasons for making them. In this way, over time, these seamless blocks of text were able to break open, once again, into poems.

I had a handful of days, in Provincetown, with the poet Stanley Kunitz, the last summer of his life. He was one hundred years old, and that summer, when anyone would visit, the time was spent reading *Moby-Dick* aloud—I would read a chapter, then he would read a chapter. Until the reading began, Stanley seemed far away, almost asleep, sunk into his chair, but as soon as the words began he came alive—I remember he especially liked the part where a sailor falls headfirst into a whale's body. It was if he were dissolving, gracefully, into pure language. I cannot imagine reading a book aloud with my father, unless it is the book I wrote about him, the only book that seems to interest him at this point. My father is constructed nearly entirely of the stories he tells about himself, each a little life raft to keep his head above the waves. He might (like Stanley), be pure language at this point (*if his story were pure enough*), yet his desire not to dissolve into it has always felt palpable (*but his story is not pure*), desperately treading the water below, anything but graceful. I tell friends (if they ask) that my father is in hospice. O, they say, then this is the end. That hadn't really sunk in, that hospice means the end.

• • •

**THE** *brain creates the mind by creating images*. . . . Damasio goes on to speculate:

> The decisive step in the making of consciousness is not the making of images and creating the basics of the mind. The decisive step *is making the images ours*, making them belong to their rightful owners. . . .

Here's an image: Dano, near the end of the film, will find De Niro sleeping outside, and hold up his hand to shield his eyes from a light. I don't know if this effect was accidental or if it was planned by the cinematographer, but it makes Dano's palm look like it is on fire. It reminds me of an offering I once made, to a lover who was living far away—I wanted to send her a photograph, I held my hand out to a mirror, and what the camera put in my palm was light. De Niro's burning hand in *The Godfather, Part Two* reminds me of this, as does the apocryphal story of Saint Columba, how he stayed up all night, the last night of his life, transcribing the last remaining Bible on earth. The Roman Empire had collapsed, marauding hordes of Huns and Visigoths were burning all vestiges of culture, swarming over what would become Europe. As they stormed the monastery walls, Saint

Columba, out of candles, lit each finger of his left hand on fire and held them aloft, so he could transcribe the Bible with his right hand. He finished at dawn, tied the manuscript to the neck of a black bird, which flew it into hiding as his door was bludgeoned open.

I don't want my father to die before we make the film about his life.

I don't want a note at the end of the film:

dedicated to Jonathan Flynn, 1929–2012.

• • •

Or do I?

# SEVENTEEN

**(2009)** Hospice. I sit and listen to him breathe. If death is the River Styx, then hospice is the boat you use to cross it. A few days later I put up two thousand dollars to lock in his cremation at a special price—this is what the brochure promises. If I wait until the day he dies it will cost two hundred dollars more. Now two men will arrive at the nursing home the morning he dies, carry his body away. The urn I pick out from the catalogue will come in the mail a week later. I get weekly updates. A woman calls, asks if he really is a famous writer. I tell her about his time in prison for robbing banks. He's a character, she tells me. Six months go by—improbably, he only seems to be improving. If he gets any better we will have to kick him out of hospice, the woman tells me. I thought this was a one-way ticket, I say. It usually is, she says. A week later I get the call—no more priest visits, no more hand-holding, no more candy stripers coming in with balloons and smiles—his one-way ticket is now a roundtrip. The movie is as far from being made as ever, and my father is still not dead.

**(2011)** At the production office the hallway to the restroom is lined with chairs, in each chair a person—an actor—hoping to play a homeless man or woman. I know that some of them are—or were—actually homeless, I got Paul in touch with them, I met them through an organization I'm connected with in New York (AIDS Service Center NYC). I look into each face in the hallway, and yes, I can imagine each as a homeless person. Even if I didn't know, I think I could tell the actors from the formerly homeless— the actors look a little too homeless, a little too wild, and the formerly homeless look a little perplexed, a little uncomfortable, yet more put-together. Again, the formula for acting drunk applies— if one is playing homeless one should try to appear not homeless, one should hold oneself with dignity. In a side room a camera is set up, a blue-green sheet hung on the wall across from it, a chair in front of the sheet. I sit behind the camera, Paul sits beside the camera, an assistant operates the camera, the casting director stands against the far wall. One by one the actors are called in.

**ONE** comes in and curls up on the floor without saying a word. One comes in with the ass of his pants ripped out—he turns and shows us, his underwear flapping as he speaks. One is supposed to be a drinking buddy of my father's, one is supposed to be the bootlegger. Each has only a line or two they've been asked to deliver—some have memorized them, some clutch onto the paper. Some need to be fed the line: *Get out of the window, you'll draw the police*, or *Hey, buddy, got a drink?* We go through them quickly—to me, they all seem good. Paul reads from his list—the bootlegger is next. The actor—Vincent—walks in, shakes all our hands. Paul turns to me: Hombre, you want to improvise a scene? Vincent, you're the bootlegger, and Nick, you're your father—you want a bottle, but you only have three dollars, and a bottle costs four. I stand up, uncertain, go stand beside Vincent. I am not, in any way, an actor. *ACTION*. I start slow, all I can think to say is, *One*, holding up one finger, meaning *one bottle*. I have three dollars in the other hand, the bootlegger can see how much I have. I'll bring you the other one tomorrow, I promise. He holds back. I reach for the bottle, he pulls it back from my hand. I offer, I cajole, I sidle up, everything short of begging. And then the next actor comes in, I'm my father again, this time telling another homeless guy about my time in prison.

I'm on a bench, looking around the shelter, above it all: Look at these guys, none of them would last a minute in federal prison, their hands out, *gimme gimme gimme*. My father, it seems, is inside of me.

**ONE** room of the production office is for props. Here is the club they will use to beat my father, here are the xeroxes of his letters on the walls, here are the bottles of vodka, and here is the tub I will find him in. A few days ago an unemployed man set himself on fire in Tunisia, today the president of Tunisia flees—WikiLeaks may or may not have had something to do with it. Then the streets of Cairo fill with protestors, and within a week the president of Egypt for the past thirty years will speak about stepping down. This will come to be known as the *Arab Spring*. Then an earthquake creates a tsunami that floods Japan, killing thousands and destroying a nuclear power plant—to this day the crippled plant is still leaking radiation, yet no one really talks about it anymore. By the time the film is finished, but before it comes out, there will be protests in every major city in the world—in America they will begin in a small park (Zuccotti) a couple blocks south of where we filmed De Niro in the snow. Tomorrow at seven the filming begins, I'm wandering the production office, everyone I know is gone for the day, the only people left in the suite of offices are people I haven't met. A girl is sitting in the empty tub as I pass, to see if her body will fit. Who are you? she asks. I just wave a hand around the room.

**ONE** part of the script troubles the studio—does my father have to be so, well, unlikable? Homophobic, alcoholic, sexist, yet especially troubling—uncomfortable—is his racism. At times he assumes black-voice (*gimme gimme gimme*); he calls a woman who works in the library an "ape." The studio wonders if Paul can cut the next-to-last scene: De Niro is off the streets, in a new apartment, Dano stops by for a visit, yet De Niro goes off on another rant, once again about how *the blacks, my African friends, rape ten-year-old white girls outside my window, day and night.* . . . It is the end of the film, and he is off the streets, yet seemingly unchanged. Is there to be no redemption?

● ● ●

I send these notes on racism (mine) to the studio:

*personal note*: My grandmother remembers that, as a child, Native Americans—Indians—would come to her back door, dressed in rags, begging for food.

*personal note*: By the time I was born there were no Indians in my hometown, either homeless or otherwise—the only Indian I ever saw was on tv, in a canoe, with a tear in his eye.

*historical note*: In my hometown there is a Cape Verdean community, they live on one street, the same street the dump is on, and when the dump got full, when it came time to find a new dump, the town voted to move it across the street.

*personal note*: When Springsteen's *Darkness on the Edge of Town* came out my friends joked that he was talking about this neighborhood. One friend's father called Martin Luther King *Martin Luther Nigger*.

*personal note*: My grandmother would flirt with Manny, who ran the dump, so that he would allow her to pick through the discarded furniture. To us, not to his face, she called him a *boogie*.

*personal note*: My grandmother always had a bowl of mixed nuts on her kitchen table from Thanksgiving to Christmas—she called the Brazil nuts *nigger toes*. . . .

*personal note*: My mother did not allow us to use the word *nigger*, not ever. Our grandmother would whisper the word *boogie* to us, even when our mother was not around.

*historical note*: In a soundproof studio Al Green is so tired, so alone, his eyes turned upward because up is his idea of heaven.

*personal note*: My mother called burning down one's own house to collect the insurance money *Jewish lightning*, though this was what she herself did, to my childhood home, while my brother and I were sleeping upstairs, and she was not Jewish.

*a note on alternative energy*: The center of the earth is on fire, the center of the earth is a planet spinning inside a planet and one of the planets is on fire.

*historical note*: If you were white and rode through Roxbury in the 1980s, a black kid might yell out, *Hey, that's my bike*, and all his friends would tumble out onto the street and chase you, try to knock you off. The only thing to do was to pedal away very, very fast.

*personal note*: Roxbury was one of the first neighborhoods I walked through when I moved to Boston, Ivan showed me around one summer day, the summer after my mother died, we were looking to score, and we did.

*personal note*: He's very articulate, my grandfather would say of Ivan, whenever he asked about him, and he always asked about him. *Very articulate* dot dot dot bracket *for a black man* end bracket.

*personal note*: One night, after working in the shelter, a couple coworkers and I were drinking a beer by the water in Southie. Some kids came up and nodded toward a Korean guy fishing nearby, told us they were going to stab him with his own knife and toss his body into the bay, asked if we wanted to watch. He's not bothering anyone, I said, and offered them a beer. I ended up in the hospital with a broken zygomatic arch (holds up the cheekbone), ten stitches in the back of my head, and a broken front tooth.

*side note*: When I tell this story some people ask what happened to the Korean fisherman, and some don't.

*side note*: In Boston a few years later I heard of a band called *Hey That's My Bike*.

# THE REENACTMENTS

*historical note*: A white man drove into Roxbury one night and shot and killed his pregnant wife as she sat beside him in the passenger seat of their Toyota. He then turned the gun on himself, grazing his stomach fat with a bullet. A recording of his desperate phone call to the police played on the news for days, *A black man just shot me and my wife*. A manhunt followed, which eventually led to an arrest, even though the police, in retrospect, all said it seemed clear the guy had done it himself. The shooter worked on Newbury Street, one of the richest streets in Boston, in a shop that sold furs—Kakas, which in Boston is how we pronounce the word *carcass*. With the insurance money, before he was arrested, while the black suspect was awaiting trial, this man upgraded his car— from a Corolla to an Acura.

*personal note*: This shooting happened when my father was in the middle of his homeless odyssey. Newbury Street is one of the streets my father spent many nights on, in doorways or ATMs or beneath church overhangs, sometimes camping out in the doorway of a fur shop that to this day, whenever I walk past, the word *carcass* comes to mind.

# EIGHTEEN

**(2011)** January, record snowfall, snow everywhere, more coming. Six weeks before shooting is to begin I get a call from Paul that De Niro wants to meet my father. He wants to go to the shelter. He wants to go the next day. It's Sunday, De Niro is in New York, I'm in Texas, due to teach the next day, my first day of classes. We can take the train up to Boston, Paul tells me, use the time to talk about the movie, about my father. He means the train from New York. I hang up and go online and book a flight. I'm on a plane in three hours. I cancel my classes.

In New York the next morning it's snowing—sleeting, really. The radio says that the trains are delayed, that the airports will close. I get a message to meet at Paul's hotel at nine, plans have changed—we are not taking the train, we will meet De Niro at an airport in New Jersey, a private airport, where a private jet will fly us to Boston. Two pilots are waiting for us, the rain has turned to snow. This is the way it is, nothing will stop us from this trip. Inside the plane it is like a yacht—leather couches, reclining chairs, enough seats for maybe six people. It's not costing us a thing, I'm told—De Niro has a credit here. I warn them that my father is much diminished, that he is not the same man as the man De Niro will be portraying—the menace is gone, he's grown old, lost his fight, toothless now.

**ON** the plane I sit across the aisle from De Niro, lean in to him as he speaks, but the engine is beside our heads and he speaks softly, so it is hard to make out the words—something about his kids, how one needs to be moved to a school closer to his home, how he is starting to have some trouble. The boy's mother, who is not with De Niro now, I assume, maybe she's in California, but I can only understand half of what he is saying. I keep flashing to his hand, wrapped in that white towel, how it pops into flame after he shoots Fanucci in the face, how he watches Fanucci fall, how only then does he notice his hand burning, how he shakes it, his eyes still on the fallen body, how the towel unwraps, how he puts the fire out. De Niro is talking to me, but I am having a hard time hearing the words. It seems as if even he is having trouble finding the right place, the right school, for his kids.

IT is impossible to know what shape we will find my father in. I worry he will be lost, incoherent. Yet when we show up at Roscommon he's awake, in the lunchroom (maybe they call it a dayroom?), and lucid. The television is on, each seat taken (The Next Holiday is EASTER). It is a grim place, though the shelter will be grimmer. My father's apartment, by the time I moved him out, was grimmer. Here he has three meals a day, he has nurses and orderlies, he is taken care of, which is perhaps all he ever desired, aside from fame. And now I am introducing him to Robert De Niro, who will play him in the film version of his life. We move to an empty room. I usually bring a copy of the memoir with me, as it seems to jog his memory (to hold it in his hands, to scan the pages that talk about his childhood, his nights in the shelter, his time in prison), but I realize I forgot to bring it. I know him so well, after writing the book, and yet I barely know him at all. I get to the edge of knowing, then teeter back and forth—that's what makes these visits shimmer. It is all we can do, all I've ever done—stand before what I know, and pulse into the unknown. For years I could not imagine what my father would be like outside of alcohol, yet here he is—he hasn't had a drink since he's been inside Roscommon. His stories are different now, not as scripted, yet in many ways the damage is done. My father is eighty—from the life he's led it's a miracle he's alive. I'd have died a hundred deaths by now, if I'd continued to drink like he drank. I forgot to bring my book, but it turns out De Niro has a copy. He pulls it out of his bag—dog-eared, heavily underlined, notes written in the margins. This is Robert De Niro, I tell my father. The actor who will play you in the film we are making about your life. My father nods, doesn't seem impressed. And this is Paul, the director—he also wrote the script. Very nice to meet you both, my father says, though he has, over the years, met Paul a few times before. I show him the book, remind him that it's about him, about his life. I point to my name on the cover—he is, as always, impressed. A book? How'd you figure that out? What promoted you? I point to the title, remind him that it's something he said, that he always was good with titles, which allows him to begin, to start talking about himself. It's like turning the handle on a jack-in-the-box, and out come his stories. Amazing that the stories are still inside him, that he can still find them. He holds forth for an hour, one tangent leads to another. When I try to bring him around to the film we're making he cuts me off: Let me speak, you wonton fucken goonball. We all smile. Paul writes *wonton fucken goonball* in his notebook. I take this moment to try, once again, to get him to take it in, that we are making a film about his life. Bob is going to play you, in the movie version of this book. That's why we're here, he wanted to meet you. He looks over at De Niro, as if taking him in for the first time. So, you do a little acting? my father asks. You like to act?

De Niro smiles, shrugs: Yeah, I do a little acting.

**MY** father is not surprised, nor seemingly impressed, that a movie is being made of his life. He has always assumed one would be, since he is the most interesting person he's ever met (*only two people can play me—either Dustin Hoffman or myself*). After asking De Niro if he liked to act, after De Niro shrugs, I tell my father, He was in *The Godfather*. *The Godfather?* my father echoes. *That's a big deal.* He narrows his eyes, takes De Niro in more fully. He *is* the godfather, I say.

**SOMETIMES,** in a movie theater, waiting for the movie to begin, the lights start to dim, gradually, and for a moment you're unsure if the room is going dark or if it's your eyes, failing. Sometimes you find yourself in a public restroom—often in an airport, on your way somewhere (where?)—standing before the automatic faucet, waving your hands, but the water does not come, the sensor doesn't sense you. Sometimes, when you try to move your cursor, the trackpad doesn't register your fingertip, the cursor doesn't move. You are both frozen—for those few moments it is as if you do not exist.

Before we leave Roscommon I take pictures of my father with De Niro, of Paul with my father, of Paul and De Niro with my father. The only camera we have is on my phone. I pass it to Paul and he takes a few pictures of me and De Niro with my father, but later I discover that none of the shots with me in them come out. Later, when I show these pictures to people, I have to explain that I was there, that that is my father, that Paul took the pictures, but something happened.

**AN** hour later, at Pine Street, no one recognizes De Niro—his hat pulled down low, he keeps covering his face with a handkerchief, as if he has a cold. I point out what I remember—the cage, the front desk, the showers, the dorm. De Niro notices that no one is walking as if beaten down, as if ashamed. Maybe this is their home, I say, or maybe if they look vulnerable they become marks. We stay for an hour or so, see what we have to see, then we go. On the plane home De Niro says that in the film he needs to be able to ramble on, to hold forth, like my father had just done with him. Two days later I hand over six pages of monologues, demented psycho ramblings, distilled versions of things my father has said to me over the years. Rants like this, when he's being thrown out of the shelter, words that will likely rattle around inside me forever:

> Where is he? FATHER MURDERER. Come out and face me. What does he know? He knows shit. He's killing himself in this cesspool, he can't even see it. Where is he hiding, in some little closet, sucking mama's tit? FATHER MURDERER. Come out and face me, coward. I could have jerked off and flushed you down the toilet. FATHER MURDERER. Face me.

# NINETEEN

**WE** weren't the kind of family to make home movies—we had no 8mm camera, the only camera we had was a cheap Kodak that sat unused in a cluttered drawer for years. I assume we simply didn't have the money, but maybe my mother's desire to erase herself meant she didn't want to leave any traces. Yet all I have left of her now is traces—a handful of photographs, some handwritten letters, ash. Life is so fucken long, I wonder why I'm still here sometimes, you know how it goes—you wonder, you push on. You call an ex-lover, knowing you might stir something up, then you call a friend who is struggling, to offer whatever help you can. You go to a play (*Death of a Salesman*), spend hours in your car, wander a saltmarsh, erase emails, whatever—when you sit down to write it all swirls around inside your head. *Attention must be paid,* sure, but running alongside this is the need—the desire—to shut off, shut down, but how? Maybe this is what killed her, this desire— quiet mind, nothingness, nirvana—which I don't believe she could ever achieve. Unfulfillable, spinning-out in the dark neighborhoods of her mind. How to step outside it, outside yourself (*get out of the movie!*), dissolve into something larger. Ocean. God. Other. If you cannot find a way to pull back the cotton wool, to see you are part of the larger pattern, what then? We all have this movie, or maybe a handful of movies, replaying in our heads, constantly. The reel, at times, is of the last night with an ex-lover, which either means you're lucky or damned, depending upon how it ended (how often do we say it ended well?). You play the last moments over and over, in the hope you can see where you went off course, but rarely is there a single moment when love, or anything, goes off course. The lights in the theater go down gradually, and each time you feel panic, then (if you're lucky) blessed—that at least you are still able to wonder if it's just your eyes.

● ● ○

*ACTION.*

In this scene Dano wakes up next to a woman who isn't his girlfriend (I wake up next to a woman who isn't my girlfriend).
Dano's head is on the pillow, his sideways face fills the screen.
All he has to do is wake up (all I have to do is wake up). *CUT.* His
girlfriend comes home a couple hours later and finds lipsticked
cigarettes beside the bed (it's fun to play such an asshole, Dano
jokes), and throws him (me) out. No, first she finds the cigarette,
then she throws book after book at him (*more Yeats, O, you're so
well read*), then he goes into the bathroom and smashes his head
into the mirror. Dano looks into his own eyes after he has
smashed it—wildness, then release. In playback the mirror
breaks over and over, all in his eyes. I never broke a mirror, no
one ever threw me out, though I did wake up beside a woman
who was not my girlfriend, over and over. I couldn't find that
part inside myself that could say, clearly, *This is wrong.* . . .

*CUT.*

**THE** first human being captured in a photograph was a man on a Paris street—the buildings stand, yet the horse-drawn carriages, as well as the other passersby, are missing, their motion leaving only ghost traces. But this one man, his boot was getting shined and so he was forced to hold his leg still, long enough for it to be captured.

His head though, his torso, is ghostly, gone.

A trailer is parked on Avenue A, the name NICK FLYNN magic-markered on masking tape, stuck to the door. But this is not my trailer, just as the one beside it, with the name JODY FLYNN stuck to it, does not mean my mother is waiting inside. I don't have a trailer—if I want to talk to Dano I have to knock on his (my) door. Dano walks up, I ask him what he listens to on his earbuds between takes. The Hold Steady, he says, and sings me a line. I ask if he knows the Heartless Bastards, I tell him I'll burn him some songs. It will be dawn inside the apartment, dawn filters have been taped to the windows. Dano will be drinking a beer and trying to write while a woman (not his girlfriend) sleeps in the bed behind him.

*Wake up, wake up*, will be his only line, as he shakes her shoulder.

**OLIVIA** Thirlby and I meet up at the Bowery Mission—Olivia is the actress who will play my (next) lover, a woman who works at the shelter, who gets me to apply for a job there. Her character is a hybrid, not based on any one woman, but several. Paul created her for the film—from stories I've told him, from his own past—just as he created my father, in some way, and me, though we are closer to being real. *I was in a pretty fucked state when I started at Harbor Street*, Olivia will tell Dano. *You should think about working there.* (In the film Pine Street will be renamed Harbor Street, a lawyer at Pine Street insisted, which I don't understand—my father is a success story, he made it off the streets alive.) In the Bowery Mission, on the walls near the ceiling of the front lobby, stretching around the room, is a quote from Matthew:

> For I was hungry and you gave me food; I was thirsty and you gave me drink; I was a stranger and you took me in; I was naked and you clothed me; I was sick and you visited me; I was in prison and you came to me.

Olivia and I are invited to sit in on a service being held in the chapel beside the dining hall—this, it seems, is the rhythm of this shelter—one prays, then one eats. I point out to Olivia that at Pine Street we had no services, it wasn't affiliated with any church—the homeless were not lambs, the workers were not shepherds—to get a meal the guests just had to line up at dinner-time.

• • •

IN the basement of a Chinese church, huddled between Jesus and poinsettias, eighteen people sit in a circle of chairs. *ACTION.* Joey Boots says, Hi, my name is Joey, I'm an alcoholic. Joey is the actor who came to the audition with his ass hanging out. *CUT.* Paul turns to me, asks, Do you have anything? I offer, It's good if they all say, *Hi, Joey,* after he says, *Hi, my name is Joey.* On the walls are framed illustrations of the Stations of the Cross—these are not props (I don't think). The camera is on its little train track again, this time aimed at Dano's face. As he listens to Joey Boots, to the airline pilot, to the morphine addict, the camera moves in closer, but they pull the lens so Dano's face stays the same size—it's trippy, as if the room were pushing into him, while at the same time falling away behind him. Dano's hair, I notice, has been dyed darker (is my hair that dark?). Jesus staggers over Dano's shoulder, his cross driving him to his knees. It doesn't matter that nothing is unfolding chronologically, that my first day working at the shelter is shot on the same day as my first 12-step meeting, and also my first time drinking on the street with a homeless guy—as Janis Joplin once snarled, *It's all the same fucken day, man.*

# TWENTY

**BEFORE** you enter the dimly lit gallery of the Glass Flowers, in a room off to the left, is a workbench (at least it was there when I first returned as an adult—it's been since moved to inside the gallery), which we are told is the actual bench used by the Blaschkas in their Dresden studio. The workbench is a butcher's block, its surface well-worn, scarred, burned in spots—It would be at home in a scientist's lab or a welder's studio. Pipettes, beakers, tongs, burners, needle-nosed pliers, petri dishes filled with sand—rough-looking, almost crude, these tools, tools that could be used to wire a house, or build a bomb—arranged, or strewn, over the surface. You would think they would be finer, like those of a jeweler (are a jeweler's tools fine?). It seems unlikely they could have produced anything as delicate as these flowers. Framed on the wall above the bench is a card for the Blaschkas, from the time before they began making flowers, offering glass eyes, and below this, in a glass case, are a few of the eyes themselves, lined up on a little shelf—they could be mistaken for marbles, if a marble could look back at us.

· ● ●

**NOW** is the day we invent the homeless, now is the day we figure out where to put them. Here is where they will eat, here is where they will line up for a bed ticket. Here is the hallway where they will linger. Here are your showers and your funhouse mirror. Here's where you undress, now hang up your clothes. Here is outside and the nowhere to go. Do you have anything for me? Paul asks after each take. I realize I'm not really here—sitting before the monitor, headphones on, gone. Can we have more black extras? I ask (again). Shelters, I point out, are as black as our prisons, but everyone knows this already.

**THE** process of making a film, I will discover, is as much of a mess as the Blaschkas' workbench. The basement of St. Patrick's has been transformed into the shower room at the shelter. Stainless steel panels are being screwed to the walls, the screws tightened just enough to distort the panels into funhouse mirrors. On the other side of the mirrored wall are where the showers would be, but there are no showers in that room, for the camera will never cross that threshold. De Niro will be in this room in two hours, in two hours the camera will be rolling. De Niro knows what he is supposed to say, but what is he supposed to do? It's his first night in the shelter—two days ago, upstairs, Dano gave him a bed ticket—but what is De Niro supposed to do with this ticket now? Who does he hand it to, and what will this person hand back to him? I walk everyone through what I remember—a worker stands behind a counter, takes the ticket, and hands him a bin. Inside the bin is a coat hanger and a wrist tag—the wrist tag has his bed number on it, this number is also on the bin, I remember now, it comes back to me as I tell it. He will put the tag on his wrist, hang his clothes on the hanger, put his shoes into the bin, then hand everything back to the worker behind the counter. The worker will have to do something with these clothes, but what? At the shelter we had a hot-room behind the counter, we hung the clothes

237

in it to disinfect them. But there is no hot-room behind this counter, so it is decided that props will need to find, or fabricate, a rolling stand to hold all the hangers. A lot can be done with duct tape. It isn't really all that different from working at the shelter, where we had to invent it all the first time around.

**ON** the wall opposite the Blaschkas' workbench are a few of the minerals used to make glass—silicate, quartz—brought in from the gem and mineral room. On this same wall is a piece of something called fulgurite (from the Latin *fulgur*, meaning "thunderbolt"), which looks like a black jag with branching roots. Fulgurite (also known as petrified lightning) is formed when lightning strikes sand—the lightning enters into the sand, travels through it, vitrifying the quartz it comes in contact with, all in less than a second. The fulgurite at the Agassiz measures about a foot, but the note says that the longest found is almost fifty feet long. The branches, apparently, are hollow, outlining the path of the lightning. It's here, I assume, to show us one way glass can be formed. A hunk of bottle-green moldavite is beside this, formed by a meteorite impact radiating its energy outward. Moldavite, fulgurite—does anyone else think these two minerals are as beautiful as any of the Glass Flowers?

**THE** *practical application of the Glass Flowers as research specimens subsided with the advent of precise color photography, plastics, air travel, and refrigerated transport. And, predictably, as the primacy of their scientific literalness receded, their role as fetish and metaphor gained power.* Here's a metaphor: A bar in Tokyo serves a cocktail made with ice said to be carved from an Arctic glacier—it is tinged faintly blue. Here's another: In a solar-powered freezer, in the center of a dimly lit room in New York City, a 4.5-ton block of ice is on display, visible behind thick glass walls—white, almost imperceptibly blue. No twigs or leaves are embedded in it—it comes from a place without trees. As you sit on the bench provided, as you walk around it, it is almost as if you've seen it before—ice, of course, but this ice, you are told, is (like that cocktail in Tokyo) carved from an Arctic glacier, cut from a place that is vanishing. If you press your hand to it, the box gives off heat; if you press your face to it, the ice will blur—a faint blue distant blur. The whole idea is that the ice will keep its shape—it won't become a glacier again, it won't become a cloud (*any day now I'll make a knife out of this cloud*). Perhaps there is a side, on top, perhaps, with frozen footprints, but this cannot be seen, not from your bench. Glaciers break off and fall into the sea, but this remnant, this chunk, will be on display forever, kept from melting by the sun.

1870—the Wares hire the Blaschkas to create the Glass Flowers. Leopold (the father) teaches his son (Rudolf) what his father had taught him (*tact increases in every generation*). My father spends his whole life writing a book (*The Button Man*) that to this day remains unpublished. I (the son) write a book (*Another Bullshit Night in Suck City*), which is, in part, the search for my father's unpublished manuscript. Focus hires Paul to create a film based on this (these) book(s). For seven weeks I go to set every day with a notebook, watch my life reenacted, take notes. When we began shooting I was writing a book about the Glass Flowers, but then the film began to speak to the flowers—both, it seems, are types of reenactments. I was also reading books on memory, on what it means to have a sense of self, how we don't really know what consciousness is made of, how we might never know. These ideas began to speak to the flowers and to the film, all of them reenactments, maybe everything is. *Remember, no matter what your eyes may tell you, they are not real. They are made of glass.* I began to see the structure of the project as a triptych—flower, film, memory—something that could be carried under the arm, unfolded anywhere, to create an altar. Not one to pray before, but one that asks, What are you feeling right now?

**FIVE** years after my father got off the streets, every few months or so, I'd go to Boston, maybe on my way to Provincetown, maybe I'd stop in to see a friend or two. I had an ex-lover who was housesitting a mansion, and part of me always wondered if we'd ever spend a night together again, in that mansion, but we never did. Often—usually—I'd end up stopping in on my father, but that wasn't the reason I went, at least that was what I told myself. As time went by, more and more I ended up making the trip just to see him, which struck me as odd, after decades when it seemed neither of us wanted much to do with the other. Now, once a year or so, on one of these runs to Boston, I go to the Glass Flowers. The last time I went, I found the exhibit had been renovated. The workbench was no longer in the anteroom before one entered the darkened room of the Glass Flowers—now the bench was tucked inside, almost as an afterthought, without context, without the glass eyes and the fulgurite, without the business card. It looked far less mysterious, almost emptied of meaning. Clearly, with the renovation, we are meant to see the flowers as art, rather than as science.

● ● ●

I wonder if my mother held my hand as we walked these hallways, past bear and badger, to the room of the Glass Flowers. Did I have to look up to see into the gorilla's eyes, just as now I have to look down? Did she lift me up so I could get a better look, just as I lift my daughter now? I am now about the size of the gorilla, but part of me is still the size of that spider monkey, clinging to its mother's back. I would like to say that I remember the Glass Flowers from that time, from before my mother went off the rails, I would like to say that the Glass Flowers fascinated me, at the beginning, but they didn't. Not when I was a child. How can a room of glass flowers, tucked away in an ill-lit room, flowers that look just like the flowers we'd passed on our way inside—daisies and goldenrod, lilac and bittersweet—how could they possibly hold my attention, when here was a real gorilla, beating its chest, snarling?

**CARVED** into the lintel over the door to the museum is the name AGASSIZ—look up as you enter and you will see it. This is why we called it the Agassiz, but it's no longer called that, perhaps because of the controversy around Louis Agassiz, its founder—apparently among his more enlightened ideas ran a vein of (white) racial superiority. His hypothesis was that if we looked closely at the flora and fauna and minerals of this world we would discover that not only were humans exceptional among all the creatures of the earth (*and God gave man dominion over all that walks and crawls and slithers*), but white humans were even more exceptional still. This idea of human exceptionalism is still rattling around in many brainpans, and may well doom us. Honeybees, I'd say, are pretty exceptional. Sequoias. Compost. Whitman had it about right: *Why! who makes much of a miracle? As to me I know of nothing else but miracles.*

● ● ●

**IN** 1976 a selection of Glass Flowers was loaned to the Steuben Glass Works in New York for an exhibition. The only way to move the flowers—the safest way—was to hire a hearse, and pack the flowers into the back where the coffins would go. As if the flowers were corpses. In 1989 the artist Christopher Williams made a series of black-and-white photographs of the Glass Flowers for a project entitled *Angola to Vietnam*. It consists of twenty-seven photographs, rearranged alphabetically according to their country of origin. *Angola, Argentina, Bolivia, Brazil, Central African Republic, Chile, Colombia, Dominican Republic, El Salvador*—countries that would come to have the worst human rights records in the twentieth century. *Ethiopia, Guatemala, Haiti.* Each glass replica of a botanical species (*Cedrela odorata, Musa paradisiaca, Ficus carica*) that Williams photographed is from a country (*Honduras, Indonesia, Lebanon*) named in the 1985 Amnesty International annual report, which documents countries where political disappearances (*Mexico, Namibia, Nicaragua, Paraguay, Peru, the Philippines*) and other human rights abuses (*South Africa, Sri Lanka, Togo, Uganda, Uruguay, Vietnam*) have taken place. *Angola to Vietnam* reminds us that these Glass Flowers were always both a Victorian and a colonial project. Each flower was a declaration, meant to represent a distant land that we (white Europeans) now owned.

245

*UGANDA, 1894*
*Blascha Model 482*
*Family, Leguminosae*
*Cajanus cajan*
*Cajanus indicus*

The United Kingdom ruled Uganda as a protectorate in 1894, the same year the Blaschkas created *Cajanus cajan*. *Cajanus cajan* is also known as the Congo pea. As far as I can tell, no Blaschka flower came from the Congo (just west of Uganda), but we do know that ten years earlier (1885) King Leopold II of Belgium declared the Congo under his protection, and by the 1890s he systematically enslaved the entire population to harvest rubber for use as tires on a new invention (the automobile). Any local who refused, who resisted in any way, or who simply did not meet Leopold's quota of rubber, was to be made an example of by having a hand chopped off. This included children. The quantity of severed hands amounted to as much as a metric ton per day, according to records kept by the Belgium protectorate. It is estimated that fifteen million people died under Leopold's protection. All we are left with is a flower that will never die.

# TWENTY-ONE

**(2011)** One of my mother's boyfriends (Travis), or the actor playing him (Billy Wirth), comes into the house we have rented in Queens. In this scene he will show me, or the actor playing me (Liam Broggy), his photo album from Vietnam. Before the camera starts rolling someone from props walks downstairs with a handgun hanging out of his back pocket, which he then puts on the table, close enough for Travis to pick up, which he will do at the end of the scene—this is the gun Julianne will use. I take a picture of the gun. Then someone calls out first rehearsal. Carolyn Forché, after spending time in Japan with survivors of Hiroshima, noted that their memory began, seemingly, after the blast. Their stories of the minutes, then the days, right after the blast were the most vivid, the most intense—even in the midst of suffering, they felt most alive. The time before the blast was distant, vague, fading, lost. Even the present moment was somehow remote, unreal. The shot is now on Julianne's shoes, wet from the ocean—she squeezes a wet towel out so the water puddles around them, but we won't see her squeezing the towel. I ask Paul if it's okay I'm here, I don't want to inhibit him, or anyone. He says, *No, no, it's good—there's a thread between Julianne and the film and you.*

● ● ●

**CERTAIN** words, those based on the thing they describe, are wired into us—a snake is called a snake because of the way it moves, the way it hisses, how it wraps around your tongue as you name it. How you become a snake when you name it. As children we watch the way our mother's mouths form the word—we need someone to say it to us first—to point to the cage, to point into the sky, to point to the snake. To say the word. A smoke machine is wheeled in, I don't know why. I ask the script supervisor (Renee), who asks the cinematographer (Declan). It's for the crack scene, he reminds us. The smoke Dano blows out will become the smoke Julianne emerges from . . . O, right, that. Certain words, for each of us, will always have more power over us than other words. I spent my first twenty years knowing every day that my mother was willing herself to stay—resisting her pills, her gun, the ocean. *Gun, ocean, pill*—I have receptors to these words inside me, we all do, but mine got lit up young, when I saw hers lighting up. *Mirror neurons*, the neuroscientists call them. *Pill, gun, ocean*. I can't pretend they aren't there, but if I don't feed them . . .

**JULIANNE** is now in the bathroom. Paul comes up as I watch the screen, but all I can see is the way the light is caught on the tiles behind her. Julianne simply sits there, on the toilet, her painkillers balanced on the sink beside her. She stares at the orange pill bottle, she must have stared at it, before she struggled off the childproof cap, before she dumped out the white capsules, before she put them inside her. A month ago on the phone I'd told Julianne that my mother took Darvon for her headaches. Today she told me that her mother would take Fiorinal—Yes, that's it, that's what she took, I'd forgotten the word (maybe she took both—she took a lot).

*Fiorinal*—it sounds like a species of orchid.

It sounds like a glass flower we forgot to make.

*ACTION.*

Julianne looks away from the pill bottle first, looks at something outside the frame, avoiding the pills, for a while. I lean over, past Paul, to see into the screen, and I get a whiff of stale beer—three glasses on the table half-filled with beer. Props? Why use real beer? A cuckoo clock calls out. Is the cuckoo clock real?

**IF** all of this is invented, if it always was, why then did we write it as if she had to die? In the documentary *The Bridge*, the filmmaker set up a camera to film people jumping off the Golden Gate Bridge—a terrible film, in all senses of the word. One jumper survived the fall, though his body shattered upon impact. As his feet left the edge of the railing, as soon as he was surrounded by nothing but air, the words *I have made a terrible mistake* rose up from inside him.

Now Julianne will go to the upstairs closet and take out her gun. It will take some time, to move everything upstairs—the camera and the lights and all the cables. Doesn't anyone know she is not going to make it? She won't make it, by nightfall I'll get the call, I'm up at college, then I'll be in a car, two friends will drive me. I'm still in touch with Nina, but Edoardo, I worry he might be dead.

I know what she will say because I wrote it—it's in the book, the book that was written a thousand years ago, the book that predicted the son would fly six hundred miles an hour one day, over rivers and mountains, that in order to do this he would have to invent the internal combustion engine, and the airplane, and the wheelie suitcase, and the cellphone, all of it, just to find her, the mother who has been lost to him for so many years. She went away one day, carved a door in the air, but it was written in the book that she would come back, that the hole would heal, that the door would close. I wrote every word, but still, so much is unknown. What will she say, what will come out of her mouth, what will be her first word? *Of god, the Kabbalah asserts: out of that which is not, He made that which is. He carved great columns out of impalpable ether.*

**IN** *Sherlock, Jr.* (a film made before he was overtaken by his "long-creeping alcoholism"), Buster Keaton plays a hapless projectionist at a movie theater. In one scene he falls asleep and dreams himself into the film he is screening. The actors in the movie become people he knows, and his dreamself moves from the projection booth into the audience, and then into the film itself—bewildered, he approaches the screen, reaches out a hand, and steps (or falls) into it. The film he enters is much like the one in the Berkeley study (*Scientists Use Brain Imaging to Reveal the Movie in Our Mind*)—the narrative broken into a series of landscapes, connected only intuitively. A garden wall becomes a mountaintop, which becomes a lion-filled jungle, which becomes a hole in a desert surrounded by cacti. Buster pulls himself from the hole as a train barrels past, and then he is back at the garden wall.

One night, a year from now, a few months after our film has come and gone from theaters, I will sit next to a poet (Kristin Prevallet) at a dinner in Rhode Island. I knew her poems, but I didn't know that in the past few years she'd become a hypnotherapist. She'd just heard me read the first few pages of this book (before it was a book), including the passage about the movie-in-the-brain (Damasio), and it reminded her of one of her treatment strategies. She places the client into a light trance state, straddling the line between the conscious and unconscious realms. The brain is constantly rewiring itself, she explains, yet often (through a traumatic event, say) the mind gets stuck in a few well-worn grooves. Sound familiar? Put yourself in a movie theater, she tells the client—the movie you are watching is the movie of what happened. Prevallet holds her palm in front of her face: This is a movie screen, tell me about the movie. At some point, as the movie is playing, Prevallet (her name, in French, means "field in a valley") tells the client to move into the projection booth (*Sherlock, Jr.*) so that he is now in control of the movie. He can edit it, slow it down, stop it, introduce new scenes. This is one very tangible, direct way to rewire your brain, Prevallet says. The amygdala tends to cluster images from a traumatic event (ocean, gun, pills), and this is a way to separate them, to allow them to once again have their own existence, outside of the story you've attached to them. I have my doubts. Even if you rewrite the trauma, even if the ocean is once again allowed to simply be the ocean, in the end she will still be dead, no? But you will be able to move on from it, Prevallet says softly. You can turn the film from color to black-and-white, from black-and-white to sepia. It can lose some of its vivid presence. But is that what I want, for her to be less vivid?

**WHAT** if she had died before the invention of film? Would I still run the movie of her death over and over in my mind, would my mind even be able to imagine it could? Or would it be more like turning the pages of a book? What if she had died before the invention of books? Would I carry her around like a triptych, set her up wherever I found myself? In the first take we don't see what she pulls from the closet. I hear Paul murmur, *The gun, a little more.* This time, when she gets the gun from the top shelf, she lets us see it—we glimpse it in her hand, in the light. I'm home for a few days from school, as I'm leaving I kiss her goodbye, but the kiss is a little wrong, a little openmouthed—she's in bed, maybe already dead, maybe just full up with pills, maybe it's a migraine, I don't know. Here comes the rain. I will know later that she had already written the first few pages of her note, that she wrote them after she read my notebook, maybe that very day. She will finish writing it a couple weeks later, while I'm back up at school. We all have a number tattooed on us somewhere—hers has come around again. I always knew she only had so much time here, I know we all do. Julianne yawns between takes, I yawn with her. I was going to take a picture of her waiting at the top of the stairs, but it is lit from below—I can't stand in her light, I can't be her shadow.

# TWENTY-TWO

**NOW** we completely fill the dead school (St. Patrick's)—we fill every dead classroom, every unerased blackboard. A year ago each room had a child inside it, seated at a little desk, learning of God, of America—that was their passion play, this is ours. That was the Son, here is the father, going down on one knee, then lower. Then he begins acting out (funny phrase, "acting out"), then the son begins to stutter, then the father gets bigger, then the son gets smaller—the father puts him in his ear, the son thinks he's gone, thinks he's invisible, thinks he is a thought in his father's head. I wear a headset, everyone is wired, I hear everything. I can hear what Dano is thinking about my hair—stringy, greasy, it falls into my face, then the sound cuts out, and I am looking into silence.

*ACTION.*

On the tiny screen I see myself reading about my father, going down. Jonathan's a little out of control tonight, Olivia says. In the next room, through those doors, De Niro's wrapped in a sheet, ranting. Dano reads the log, then he closes it, walks through those doors, toward De Niro. But he won't come through the other side of those doors for a couple days, we need to build the lobby first.

● ● ○

**THE** film has always been an experiment, where the man (me) with the missing arm (mom) is put into a mirrored box, so that what his mind sees is his body, complete again, before the disaster. The mind refuses to believe the arm is gone, all these years it's bothered him—the itch, the ache, constant—the other hand reaches for it, the fingers close on nothing.

Now Captain (Wes Studi) is bringing Jonathan up for barring. The shelter workers sit in a circle of chairs as one reads the log out loud, an entry about Jonathan not getting any better, *in fact he's getting worse.* It's time to encourage him to find help elsewhere. All in favor of barring? On the screen the hands go up one by one, the hands go up all around me. Peter denied Jesus three times, washed his hands three times. Weren't you the one with the prophet yesterday? he is asked. He has nothing to do with me, I say—he's just a con man and a drunk. I watch the hands go up. All opposed? I'm hollowed out, I'm insulated, I'm behind the cotton wool, and on the other side is the vote, on the other side is my father, put out in the cold. Dano asks Paul something about the shot. I dig it, Paul says, when I watch your face I'm thinking of how synapses fire. Jesus comes back to the upper room: Peter, do you love me? (You know I do.) Then feed my sheep. Then be the rock.

**THIS** is the day De Niro comes into the shelter for the first time, looking for a room, or at least a bed. Dano is working the Cage, handing out bed tickets, seeming to enjoy the work. I enjoyed the work. Then the moment of recognition—De Niro stands before him, the cage between them—there must have been a moment. We film twenty takes. First the camera is on Dano's face, he makes each take different—shock to a twisted smile to rage to something ineffable. I like them all. Then we turn it around—the same scene, but now the camera is on De Niro. De Niro asks for a room twenty more times, each take different. If it were my film I'd use every take, I'd make a whole movie out of this one moment, out of De Niro asking, Do you have a room for the evening? Out of Dano saying, You want a bed? I'd repeat it over and over, one take bleeding into the next. You want to know how I felt? Here, here is how I felt.

*CUT.*

● ● ●

**NOW** we are in the cafeteria, dinnertime at the shelter, the scene of a hundred extras, the Cecil B. DeMille day. Startling how easy it is to find extras who look homeless—we don't even have to dress them. It's De Niro's first meal at the shelter, Dano comes in and sees him eating. It took awhile to get everyone eating. One guy stands behind Dano, leaning against the wall away from the others—I suggested to Paul that he stand there, someone always holds himself apart. Maybe he's a psych guest, maybe he can't sit with the others, maybe he has to hold himself apart, maybe that's what will save him.

**DE** Niro is wrapped in a sheet, barefoot in a pool of his own piss, ranting in a blackout. He stands in the middle of the now-empty cafeteria, the tables folded up and pushed to the sides for the night. Get this into your head at once, he rants—I'm a great artist. A few men sprawl out on mats on the floor—my father is now among those who cannot make it upstairs. Now he is losing even this— the chance to line up, the chance to be woken at five—maybe this, somehow, is what will save him. It was only by being kicked out of the shelter that he survived, by tasting how desperate one can become, though he just as easily could have died out there. This moment he is, unwittingly, sacrificing himself for me, by going there first: This is where you will end up, this is how it will look, unless you change your life. Dano has to simply walk through the doors, to look at De Niro, to will himself to linger, listen. In real life I saw my father hold his cock, wild in his hand, and piss on the floor of the Brown Lobby. De Niro will not take out his cock, the piss is just water, colored yellow, carried in a plastic jug. De Niro points to Dano: You, without faith you are lost, without faith you are nothing. You. Are. Nothing. Nothing. Dano takes it in, walks away, he doesn't break down, he doesn't pick up a chair and break it over De Niro's head. He brings it inside, where it can transform him. But it will take years.

**WE'RE** between shots. Jerry, who does De Niro's hair, asks me if I know someone named Peter _____. It turns out that Jerry lived in Boston when I did, that he used to stop by Pine Street from time to time to drop off donations, to look around. His uncle Peter wandered off in the early sixties, ended up living on the streets, he thought he might find him there. That scene we shot last week, Jerry tells me, with the homeless guy getting beaten to death— that was how Peter died. I ask if he has a photo—he does but it is from the fifties. He was tall, Jerry says—something happened. An extra (Carl), as he lies in his shelter bed, calls me over—he doesn't have a speaking part, he's "background." How did I look in that shot? Carl asks. Did you see how I was moving my neck as if I was hurt? We've talked off and on throughout the shoot, he's told me that the days he doesn't get called in he eats at food pantries—not for research, but because he's broke. It's why I want to be here, Carl tells me—I know this, I know what this movie's about. Another extra tells me she needs to work two more days this year to keep her SAG health benefits, asks if I can put in a good word. Radioman has been waiting outside for the past two days, hoping for a part—his nickname comes from the boombox he wears like a necklace. Radioman claims Robin Williams based his character for *The Fisher King* on him—to look at him, it could be true.

**AFTER** lunch we will move to just behind the cafeteria walls. De Niro now wears his final coat, the tore-up blue down jacket with the feathers slipping out. Time has passed, he's about to find out he's been barred (*father murderer*). I'm sitting just on the other side of the wall, watching the monitor, as De Niro tries to come inside. Snow follows him inside. Two shelter workers, Carlos (Eddie Rouse) and Gabriel (Victor Rasuk), block his way, ask him to leave. Jonathan, you're barred, you can't come in. De Niro will not leave easily, I'd warned Victor and Eddie—he will fight you. Does my son know about this? De Niro asks, barely taking the workers in. He knows, *cabrone*, you got to go. De Niro improvises the lines, adds my name—Nicholas, where are you? Nicholas Flynn, *FATHER MURDERER*, come out and face me. I don't need the headphones to hear him call my name—he is just behind this wall.

• • •

**HERE'S** the day that never happened, here's the day I invite my father inside my apartment and we have a talk about my mother (I never invited my father inside). In the business this is what is known as an *obligatory scene* (a scene the viewer waits for and excitedly looks forward to). Today is my mother's birthday, she'd be seventy today. If her last attempt had failed, if she didn't get to that place again, if she made it out (*I have made a terrible mistake*). Today is the day of the burning palm, today I get to bring my father inside, after I find him under a bush, asleep. This is what the whole movie is about, this moment—the father sleeping outside, the river flowing beside him, beside us—the river, of course, is my mother, and what she did, and how we keep trying to leave it. By taking my father inside, I am able to tell the story of the notebook, the one my mother read. The incomplete story I wrote, the story without an end. I left off the end, then it ended. My mother read it and then she ended. I take a picture of a chandelier, how it hangs over us, watching us talk about self-hatred. We will get it right by sundown. Julianne will return on Monday, as a ghost.

● ● ●

**AFTER** five takes Dano murmurs to me, I can't figure out why he'd invite his father inside—I know it's not because he's a good guy. I smile, ask why it always takes him five takes to get it right. *When I did it I nailed it on the first take, every time.* This is the scene where Dano admits to De Niro that he thinks he has a drinking problem, and De Niro says, A drinking problem? That's problematic. This, I realize, is a hinge—one of many—that opens a door. Now Dano has nothing to lose, he is now free tells the story that has yet to be told, the story of night the mother died. A second hinge is when De Niro says, The question is not why she died when she did, the question is why she stuck around as long as she did. This is why Dano brings De Niro inside, why Paul wrote it as he did, to release this energy. I didn't see it when I read the script, only when I heard them speak the words. In life it took twenty years to release this energy—I spent each day, for twenty years, trying to unlock this door, but each morning I'd find it, once again, locked.

**ONE** more day with Liam, the actor who plays me as an eleven-year-old (my inner child). A month has passed since we first met. Liam is writing now, a book about the apocalypse. All the food is gone, and people have gone crazy, except for one man, a Native American, but Liam can't figure out his weapon. I suggest a bow and arrow. Liam is thinking blowpipe. His mother (Stacy) tells me that their family is not unfamiliar with my father's story. She tells her story as a call-and-response with Liam. Your cousin was where? In prison, Liam answers. Why? He stole a computer from a friend he worked with, Liam answers. He stole from everyone, Stacy says, even me. The story involves drugs and penny stocks and prostitution, or something like prostitution, but by now Stacy is talking in code, yet I'm sure Liam knows exactly what is being said, since he is who I was.

**THE** loneliness of the actor between scenes, chewing her nails, wondering if she found it. Found what? Something beyond the realm of understanding, the word inside the word, the emotion inside the emotion. The hinge. I want to tell her she's perfect, but it's not for me to say. In eight days my life will end, at least this version of it. In eight days this one story from my past will become pure light. Ryan (props) holds a crack pipe out to me, asks if it looks okay, if it looks real. I don't want to touch it, I don't want to take it in my hands. He'd described it to me first—a glass straw with a brillo pad in one end for a screen. That'd work, I say. Any fucken thing works—glass stem, apple, tinfoil—whatever gets that shit inside you. I don't really even remember what mine looked like. I remember a room and a guy with a lighter, I remember passing him a twenty for each hit—or maybe it was two hits for twenty, maybe I emptied my pockets after the first hit—either way we were going through it, we were spending the night in that room, the party raging (full-on) just beyond the door. I don't remember his face, only what he said—*Don't*—just before I took the first hit. When Paul edits these scenes he will cut a scene of Liam eating ice cream between the scenes of Dano taking hit after hit of crack, and I will think, *Yes, ice cream, perfect.*

● ● ●

**RAIN** today, we can see our breath, the street covered in fake snow. De Niro is in his final outfit, the same outfit we first saw him in, back in January, on the first day (my birthday). In film time it's the morning after the night I took my father inside. De Niro has woken up, left without saying goodbye. Dano has followed him out onto the street, calls after him, Where are you going? I'm going to my suite at the Ritz, De Niro tells him. Then he turns, comes back: Out of curiosity, why haven't you ever asked me to stay with you before? Here it is again, another hinge—something heretofore unknown or as yet unarticulated, made manifest. Why haven't you taken me in before? It is raining still, cold. We see Dano's breath. Did I ever see my father's breath? Did I ever see him breathing? Dano calls De Niro a drowning man, De Niro turns, comes back, sneers, A drowning man? A drowning man? I'm not a drowning man. The hours fold into themselves, the shot keeps getting retaken, the camera moves from wide to tight. Then everything turns around and we go through it all again, looking for something ineffable. De Niro says, I'm not your poor mother, I'm not going to die out here. I'm a survivor. Dano doesn't understand why he doesn't punch him. I explain that he has found one of the glitches, a spot where we have messed with reality. My father said these words to me, but he was outside my locked gate when he did, and it was snowing, and he was on his way to nowhere. I didn't have to punch him, I simply didn't open the gate.

**DAY** thirty-six—for the past three hours we have been filming Mom, Dad, and me. This is the first time we are all together since I was born. In this scene Julianne appears in the shelter, standing between De Niro and Dano. She turns, looks at one, then the other, smiles, then vanishes. Declan shoots her standing, and then he shoots her gone—she simply walks out of the frame when the camera pans to Dano's face, and when it pans back she is gone. She was never really there, she is a dream, a ghost, but we both see her, everyone sees her. After the first shot Paul turns to me and says, This is the hinge, the word I'd murmured to him on Friday. I don't know if this is the hinge, I don't know if a hallucination can be a hinge. Then come the close-ups, tight on each actor's face, as they take in the apparition, as the apparition takes them in.

**DAY** forty—we are in my father's apartment, the one he moves into after he gets off the streets. A bottle of vodka on the kitchen table. You got anything for me? Paul asks. I point to a bottle of whiskey holding up some books on his desk—my father's not the kind of drunk who has an extra bottle around for bad days or to offer a friend a drink. He buys a bottle of vodka and he drinks it. Then he buys another, over and over, until the money runs out. Tom removes the bottle. Paul asks if he would have made his bed—the bed here is made. I think it looks too neat. Paul thinks he's been institutionalized so he would make it, but I think prisons and shelters have left him more infantilized—you don't make your own bed at Pine Street. The bed looks too good, I say, the pillows too clean, the blanket too new. Maybe even the fridge is too clean, but maybe not—this is early on in this post-homeless apartment, it hasn't yet disintegrated, hasn't yet dusted over, hasn't collapsed in on itself. Tom messes up the bed a bit. *ACTION.* Dano knocks on the door. Paul thinks he played it too dead in the first take, but I think he *is* dead at that moment, seeing the father he left for dead. I think Dano nailed it, first take, which is all we really get, all we are allowed, after today. Tomorrow we fold up the tent and move on. It's dusk inside, but the door to this stage opens to sunshine.

# TWENTY-THREE

I ask Kristin Prevallet, the same night we meet, if she can hypnotize me. I want to enter the theater. I want to change (or at least try to change) the movie. Later that night she gives me a brief session. Following her instructions I open and close my eyes while looking at a white wall, extend my peripheral vision, relax my body. It feels like meditation. Do you see a movie theater? Yes, I see it. Are you in it? Yes. Is a movie playing? The theater is enormous, baroque, the screen is white. It is empty except for me. Is it supposed to be empty? I ask. That's up to you, she says. I'm alone in a dark theater. The screen stays white. Let's try something else, she says. You are in a boat, a plumb line is tied to the boat—lower your body into the water with the line tied to you. I see the boat, I see the line tied to my waist, I drop into the water. Sink deeper, you are safe, you are still connected to the boat. In seconds I am at the edge of an even deeper drop-off—my body freezes. The line is no longer taut, it's coiling behind me, bunching up. I can go no further into this blackness, this Thanatos, the place my mother went to—*pure death, self-destroying*—I cannot follow, not with my body. Can you look into it, can you describe it? Prevallet is simply a voice now, perhaps her voice has become the line I can follow back to the boat, if I need to. I am now sinking into the blackness, now up to my knees in it. My body twitches. Is it mud, or space, or darkness? the voice asks. Space, I answer—no, mud. No, it's all three. Even

275

as I name it I am in it, yet not in my body. I am now simply breath, my body gone. I am sorry I've left you, I say, I don't know how to bring you through this. My breath then, imperceptibly at first, begins to make a tunnel through the darkness, dissolving the utter black into gray. Just before the voice asks if there are any colors I glimpse violet, tingeing everything. And as I think the word *violet* I know I have a mind, and as I see violet I know I have eyes, so my body must be somewhere. Her voice moves me through the gray now, now I'm floating above a canyon—yellow walls, sandstone. Her voice asks, What is below the yellow? Green, I see green. Go to it, she says, and I go. On the green is my body, waiting. I want to rest here, but her voice asks, What is below this? And the green gives way to blue, and below this the blue gives way to white— cold, cold white. I do not want to go into this white—this is the place my father got to, sleeping outside all those years, waking up covered in snow. I don't know if I will survive, I barely survived seeing his body covered in snow—then I am in it, her voice places me in it, inside it my body trembles, a pain shoots through my foot. The voice asks, How can you get out of it, do you see  a way out? As I hear these words I am moving through a tunnel, the walls white, cold, yes, still, yet like folds of flesh, and then I'm out-side of it. You can open your eyes whenever you want to, Prevallet says.

● ● ●

**MY** instinct when I visit the Glass Flowers now is to keep reminding myself that they are glass, even though it is impossible to forget this. *Please do not lean on the cases. All the models are made of glass.* The petals of the tulips, the hairs on the stems of the peach branch, the blossoms which seem only a god (or an ant) could have opened. On some of the plants there are even imperfections—fungus, rot, insects eating away at the leaves—just as it is in the fields. Rudolf, the son, added in the rot, perhaps as a way to acknowledge what his father, in his perfection, left out. Yet even the rot is contained, it has to be, frozen in that moment—none of these flowers will rot further, they will not return to earth, not as long as the Agassiz stands.

●  ●  ●

**WHAT** is this desire to capture the world, to hold on to it forever? The glass flowers are erotic (open, wet), yet encased in glass, like little televisions. Like pornography. You cannot smell them, you cannot touch them. I've spent part of the last three years convincing my child not to rip every flower she sees from its stem, not to crush their petals between her fingers. What is this impulse? I'm far from immune from it, I sometimes join her in the destruction—absentmindedly I'll pluck a flower and tear it apart, barely clocking what I'm doing. With her, I try to point out when the flowers are not ours, in a public planter, say, or a stranger's garden—more a part of the universe.

**OUT** of that moment Jesus was nailed to his cross flowed our attempts to represent it, to create a narrative that could contain it. Yet the body, hanging there, is still, simply, terrible. Caravaggio's genius was to paint Jesus with dirty feet, to bring him back down to earth. Rudolf (the son) put decay and fungus back onto the leaves, thereby elevating the Glass Flowers above kitsch. His father had to die for him to see that the perfect peony in bloom is less interesting, less real, than the ant-covered peony bud. We wake up in trying to understand the ants, they force us to pay closer attention. *The moment one gives close attention to anything, even a blade of grass, it becomes a mysterious, awesome, indescribably magnificent world in itself.* The peony is no longer merely pretty, it now contains struggle, and we can finally understand that all these flowers would be gone, if not captured. Yet is it enough? The workbench is compelling because it juxtaposes a jar of glass eyes with a blue petal, the petal revealing its armature. Our eyes look at those eyes as those eyes look at us. Would it help to have a vase of dead flowers as you enter, or a bowl of rotting fruit, so you could smell the decomposing, so that you couldn't forget this is a trick? Would it help to know that the flowers themselves, the very glass they are made of, is also decaying? *See the white powdery stuff on the leaves? This is glass corrosion.*

I have a friend, a writer (Kelle Groom) who, when she first heard me read from this book, could not understand the concept of the mirrored box. Afterward, try as I might, I could not explain the process to her, how it worked, how it tricked the brain into healing. All she could imagine was a mirror, reflecting back the face of the sufferer. When she heard the word *mirror* she saw her own face, and as I tried to describe it she saw a hall of mirrors, where the whole body, along with the missing arm, was reflected back, endlessly. Talking with her I realized that a mirrored box could just as easily reflect a body with both arms gone, that the movie could go either way.

For over thirty years now my brother has had, apparently, no desire to meet our father—the years our father was living on the streets and in shelters he had no desire to engage with him at all (not that I had an overwhelming desire—he simply showed up at my work and didn't leave). Over the seven weeks of the shoot my brother comes to set a handful of times (just because he has no desire to meet our father does not mean he has no desire to meet Robert De Niro), where he is given his own chair before the monitors, his own set of headphones. Now he gets to see what it was like for our father to sleep outside, now he gets to encounter our father sleeping out. But he does not come on our days with Julianne.

Last night Maeve woke me up, crying. I went to her bed, to

comfort her. Where are we? she asked. We're in your room, I told her, everything's all right. Why is the movie so dark? she asked, staring up at the ceiling. Why is it so scary? The room did seem especially dark—maybe there was no moon. I laid my head beside hers, looked at the ceiling with her. What's the movie, I asked, what do you see? A snake is biting my leg, she said, her voice rising again. Make it stop. I looked at the ceiling. Is it just one snake? I asked. Lots of snakes but only one of them is biting me. Make it stop, she repeated. Can you change the movie, I asked, can you tell the snake to stop? Can you make the snakes go back into their holes? Can you make the sun come up? Can you see any flowers? She was quiet for a moment, wide-eyed. It's a little lighter, she said. Any flowers? A few red flowers, she said. Any snakes? Snakes are all asleep now, she said softly. Maybe we can go back to sleep ourselves? I offered.

Why did you give me these eyes? she asked, as she drifted off.

**IN** the original Greek the sense of the word *catharsis* was as a daily practice—we woke up each day with who we were, with our particular sorrows and struggles, and each day we had to find a way to carry through. This contrasts with our more contemporary idea of catharsis as a onetime event, a revelation—a light coming on in an empty room. In this version, once we find the switch to turn that light on, we then get to see clearly what it was in our past (hi, Mom) that causes us to act the way we do—we are then, ideally, able to integrate it (her) into our lives, and we are healed. Or, if it were a daytime television show, we'd watch as others act out their scripted feelings: *On today's show we have a man who slept with two sisters and neither one knew. And we have both sisters with us.* When the sisters come out the audience cheers (is there an applause sign that lights up?). When the man comes out the audience hisses (maybe we are past that point now?). The women are allowed one, maybe two, emotions—betrayal? anger? love? The man can either be contrite or resolute. Then we take a commercial break. What have we learned? Do you now know what to feel when you find out your lover has been fucking your sister? Think of coming home one day, to blood on your kitchen floor. Now kneel down and clean it up with a sponge, watch as it whirlpools down the drain. How does that feel? It depends on whether you think *apple* or *fast car* when you see red, or whether you (my bull) see red when you see red—either way, it will never transform this blood into an apple.

# TWENTY-FOUR

**SOMEONE** yells, *ROLLING*, and everything stops. All one hundred workers stop—teamsters and carpenters and grips and extras—stand as if frozen, eyes straight ahead. Not talking, simply being. Cars flagged down on the corner, pedestrians asked to pause. Julianne stands alone in the middle of our living room. Outside, the world has stopped, really stopped—like the film *Paris Qui Dort*, where a scientist invents a raygun that freezes the entire city—until Paul yells, *CUT*. What if this were the way it was—hair and makeup, twenty takes, someone to wrap a towel around her shoulders when she comes in soaking wet, someone to hand her a coffee, someone to read over her note with her, to help her write it? Later, Paul will hire a songwriter (Damon Gough) to write the soundtrack to it all, but no song was playing, no song would play for years after, none I could hear. All I could hear were cars backfiring in parking lots, all I could hear were hammers in the woods. If she could hear a song, then it won't happen. If she could read her own handwriting, it won't happen. If she could look at the pills as they spill out onto the counter, it won't happen. This is the worst day of the shoot, I tell anyone who asks, but no one asks. That's not true—Paul asks, Caroline (the line producer) asks, but then she touches my thigh and it feels like an electric shock. After this, seeing De Niro play my father will be easy, after this everything will be easy, and it was, when I think about it. After she died everything was easy.

*THE* *decisive step in the making of consciousness is not the making of*
*images and creating the basics of the mind. The decisive step is mak-*
*ing the images ours, making them belong to their rightful owners....*
The decisive step. A handgun the police confiscated and never
returned. A nightgown, heavy with blood, curled on the carpet.
An empty orange pill bottle, searching for its white childproof
cap. It has never been my problem to make these images mine—
the problem is that I'm haunted by them. A five-page handwritten
note that by the last page is almost impossible to decipher. A rag
I wring out into a white sink, a pink swirl down the drain (it might
have been the first time I wondered where the sewers led—to the
sea?). A white wooden chair with its back blown out, the last
piece of furniture my mother's body would touch. I never fix the
chair, I can't, it becomes a stool, I carry it with me from apartment to apartment, for ten years. It ends up holding a jade plant
my mother had given me in high school—what have I done, what
have I ever done, but make these images mine?

**EACH** of us, at birth or maybe at some point in our early child-hoods, is given a handful of images—our job, throughout the rest of our lives, is to try to make sense of them. Robert Frost offers this: *The whole great enterprise of life, of the world, the great enterprise of our race, is our penetration into matter, deeper and deeper, carrying the spirit deeper into matter.* For Jung, *If you possess the image you possess half the thing itself.* These images, these objects, are mediums of what Freud and Breuer (in *Studies on Hysteria*) called *besetzung* (occupation), which when translated became *cathexis* (from the Greek *to hold fast, to occupy*). Cathexis is the investment of our emotional energies—our anxieties, our fears, our lust, our hopes—into objects (or persons, or ideas), in order to contain these anxieties. Cathexis functions, then, like a totem object, like a fetish. Once contained we can then pass these anxieties, these energies (literally) on to another, which may (or may not) bring about catharsis, in that other.

After lunch we go into the bedroom, to align the body. For this we use Julianne's stand-in. Someone had asked her, earlier, as she sat at the dining room table, if she knew what she was doing. I'm supposed to look suicidal, she answered, and the room laughed. Paul stands over her now as she lies on the bed, then asks her to get up so he can show her what he's thinking. Facedown, he twists his arm awkwardly behind his head, crosses his legs. Then he rises, and the stand-in takes his place, arranges her body like he had done. Christo (first assistant director) comes into the room, points to a spot on the blanket beside her body. So you want blood here, pooling? he asks Paul. And here, on the back of her dress? The sun is down, Christo glances at me. Some part of me wants to say, I made it through the real day, of course I can make it through this, but everyone knows I didn't make it through, not really.

She shot herself in the chest, right? Christo asks Paul.

In the heart, I want to say.

**ACCORDING** to Freud, the "compulsion to repeat" the trauma—be it in art, nightmare, or waking life—is the organism's attempt to master the surplus anxiety that the original incursion produced, yet this cycle of repetition can, of course, lead one down the same rabbit hole, over and over, with disastrous results. Or it can offer a glimmer of empathy. Sometimes (mostly) it simply leads to both. *Get out of the movie, fuckhead.*

The next day I want to call Paul. It hadn't occurred to me earlier, but the force of the blast would have blown—did blow—out her back. It left a bullet-sized hole in her chest, but the back, the exit wound, was gaping. Like a bullet through an apple. The chair she had sat herself in, its spindles all blown out.

I hadn't told Paul about the chair.

# TWENTY-FIVE

**ONE** theory states that the universe created man so that it would have someone to contemplate it—it was unable to contemplate itself so it created us. Then, after a half-century search, physicists discover a subatomic particle—the Higgs boson, or the "God Particle"—which might answer the questions, Why are we made of matter rather than simply light? Why is there something rather than nothing? The *New York Times* weighs in: *The finding affirms a grand view of the universe described by simple and elegant and symmetrical laws—but one in which everything interesting, like ourselves, results from flaws or breaks in that symmetry.* Flaws or breaks in the symmetry—hasn't it always felt this way, haven't we believed this all along, that these flaws, these breaks, are what made us? In the midst of tears and celebration, even the physicists know that this discovery is simply a threshold. The whole universe awaits.

Eagleman offers this: *One of the seats of emotion and memory in the brain is the amygdala—when something threatens your life, this area kicks into overdrive, recording every last detail of the experience. The more detailed the experience, the longer the moment seems to last.* The moments after my mother died (a "flashbulb moment") seemed to last an eternity, yet the way she went away was too fast, too sudden—I might relive it constantly, yet my mind was never able to take it in, not fully. I was offered a choice—yes or no—to be on set to see it reenacted. What would you have done? And so, for the past several months, hundreds of people—the crew, the actors—have woken up every morning before the sun, built rooms that we could enter into, filled a trailer with costumes, printed up the scenes for each day on little half sheets, all this so that she would come back, if briefly, like a star, whose light we all know is dead, yet it's still so bright, until it falls, and then is gone forever. *I dragged myself to the ocean but I couldn't throw myself in*, she wrote, with this hand. I look at my hand as I write these words. How hard was it to drag myself here today? Walking from the car to set I couldn't feel my feet. I said to myself, I can't feel my feet. I need to feel the sidewalk, I said—I need to feel my feet on the sidewalk. The old stuff is really hard to erase, Eagleman says.

● ● ●

**IMAGINE** you're in an airplane, looking out the window at whatever it is below. Sometimes you can't tell if you're looking down on the tops of clouds or mountains—each housing development could be a graveyard, each river could be a pulse. Someone on the radio just said that one-quarter of the earth's land is now so polluted as to be unable to produce anything—can that be true? One-quarter of the earth? The universe is now believed to be made up of 83 percent dark matter, and we don't know what it is. We can only describe it by what it isn't, by the light it takes in and never releases. There will always be days like this, when you have to exist in uncertainty for longer than seems bearable. My friend Alix knows a bankrobber who did time in solitary—Joe _____. He went into the hole and lay there alone for a month, for two. When he first entered that darkness he was angry—murderously angry—and as he lay there all he could feel was that fuse of rage. As the days passed he lay there and he felt it and at some point he began to follow it, inside him, like a rope leading out of a well he'd fallen into a long time ago, and as the days passed he was able to trace the origins of his anger back to its source. He saw where it began, he held it, and as he lay there in the dark longer it lost its power, it began to fade, until it dissolved in his hands. His own mind had created his own hell, all these years. If

it's true that we create the world by the precise level of our attention to it, or if it exists all along with or without us, I still don't
know. More than likely it hovers, like everything, somewhere
between these poles.

**A** year from now, after our film has come and gone from theaters, I'll make the trip to Boston to show it (on DVD) to my father. It's one hundred degrees when I pull in to Roscommon, I find my father in the day room, with the rest. The woman in charge of activities (Iris) asks my father if he knows who I am. He looks at me blankly. Do you know who Nicholas Flynn is? she asks. Nicholas Flynn? That's my son. That's me, I say, and he turns and takes me in. I have two sons, he tells me. I know, I say, I'm Nicholas. The woman across from us recognizes me, and I recognize her—her name is Mary. Mary rolls her eyes when my father tells me my own name. You look like my cousin Brenda, she tells me. Three other women are at my father's table, I recognize them all—Dorothy, Josephine, Carol. It's two in the afternoon, everyone gets popsicles, but not my father (special diet, aspiration danger). I ask Iris if we can put the DVD on the flat-screen, which is turned up very loud. We turn off Oprah, slide the DVD in. I point to the screen. That's De Niro, I tell my father, he's playing you—my father looks confused. I remind him about the time they met. O, yes, he says, I remember. A few minutes later Paul Dano appears, lying in bed. His voiceover tells us, *I'm just trying to wake up.* I look over at my father, to tell him that Dano is me, but my father has nodded off to sleep.

I return the next morning, at ten o'clock, when I know he will be awake. He is back in the dayroom.

Today is
FRIDAY
JUNE 22, 2012

I sit down next to him, ask, Do you know a Nicholas Flynn? Tricky Nickie, my father says. He's my son. The television is loud. I offer my hand, tell him to give me a firm handshake. I'm your son, I tell him. O, he says. What's your name? Nicholas Flynn, I tell him. You're Nicholas? I ask Iris if we can turn down the television, but today we cannot turn it down. We're about to have a sing-along, Iris tells me. I set up my computer on the table in front of my father and slide the DVD in. Iris hands out xeroxed packets of songs, and the sing-along begins: *Birds are singing, for me and my gal.* I pull the computer closer to us, lean into my father, point to the screen. That's Robert De Niro, playing you when you drove a taxi in Boston. He's a hot-looking shit, my father says. Dressed well. America has produced only three classic writers, De Niro's voiceover tells us—Mark Twain, J. D. Salinger, and me. I'm Jonathan Flynn. Everything I write is a masterpiece. I repeat what De Niro just said, and my father nods. The other fourteen people in the room sing, *In love-land, for me and my gal.* I lean in closer, plug in my earbuds, try to put one in my father's ear, but he bats it away. What are you doing? he barks. We are put on this earth to help other people, Dano parrots, and a few moments later he gets punched in the face. I just got punched in the face, I tell my father, pointing to the screen. Seriously? my father asks. I point to each actor, say, That's Nick Flynn, your son. he says, Nicholas Flynn, That's my son. I say, I'm Nicholas Flynn, and my father glances at me. O yes, he says. I point to the other actors as they appear: That's Jody, your wife. That's you. This is Al. O, yes, my father says, each time. *Five-foot-two, eyes of blue*, everyone but us sings. Diamond rings and all those things.

### The season is
### SUMMER

Many are in wheelchairs, one woman's hair is dyed bright red. *Has anybody seen my girl?* Now Olivia Thirlby is reading the letters my father sent me from prison. That's Jessica, I tell my father, and he says, Jessica? She was always kind, he says. Olivia reads, Punch drunk, dead drunk, mean drunk. . . . What is this? she asks. A poem, Dano tells her. *When Irish eyes are smiling*, our chorus sings. It's shit, Dano tells her, no one will ever read it. *Sure to take your heart away.* I just did, Olivia mutters.

### The weather is
### HOT and [a drawing of the sun]

This is you, I tell my father, you have been evicted from your apartment. You were sleeping in your cab, and now this is your first night sleeping outside. De Niro is in a library, writing a letter. The poor and the hungry are our constituents, De Niro's voiceover tells us. Then the library closes, and De Niro is in a coffee shop. That's you having a cup of coffee, I tell my father. Now? he asks. In the movie, I tell him. You have no place to sleep, you're going to have to sleep outside tonight. That's not unusual, my father tells me. *Tiptoe through the tulips*, the room sings. Bare feet, my father says. What? I ask. He's looking over at Iris, who is singing, *Tiptoe through the tulips*, her shoes kicked off. Beautiful legs, my father says.

The next holiday is

FOURTH OF JULY

[a drawing of a flag]

Now De Niro walks through the snow to the blowers. Here's the blowers, I say. Behind the library, remember? You're going to spend the night on the blowers. Recently? my father asks. A few scenes later we are in the shelter. This is Pine Street, I tell him. The Pine Street Palace, he sneers, leaning in closer to the screen. Where is the shelter kept? he asks. I look at the screen. Fake snow is falling. You slept outside for a couple months, then you went to the shelter. To get a bed. That's where you and I will meet. That's nice, my father says. We watch for a couple moments in silence. Our chorus sings, *You are my sunshine, my only sunshine*. Where did you get this thing? my father asks. You mean the computer? He looks back at the screen. Is this the one in the South End? he asks. Is it still open? It's still open, I tell him. Now Dano is talking to De Niro through the mesh of the cage. He works at Pine Street, I tell my father, he's upset that his father is staying there. I would think so, my father says. Why? I ask. It's a tough situation, he says. These few words are more than we have ever spoken to each other about what those days were like for him, for us. You slept in the shelter for a while, I remind him, then you slept outside. That was bad, my father says, all bravado gone. *You make me happy when skies are gray*. What was bad? I ask. Sleeping outside, my father answers. But the shelter wasn't exactly paradise.

When it's over I stand, close the computer, take his hand. I have to be somewhere, I tell him. I'm already pushing it. Where will you go? my father asks. Rhode Island tonight, I tell him. I'm doing a reading. What will I do? he asks. In his mind he's back on the streets, back in the years he slept outside, I know this. You'll stay here, I tell him. Lunch is coming. When? my father asks. Right now, I say.

**PHANTOM** limb pain is pain someone feels over something that is no longer there. (*Let's return to the scene of the fucken tragedy, at least we all know how it turns out, instead of this endless uncertainty. . . .* ) The one way, the only way (so far) we've found to relieve this pain is through a resurrection—you step into a mirrored box, which makes it look like your missing arm has come back. The mind has had such a hard time understanding—the arm (my fucken *arm?*) is gone—it might never understand. But inside the box the body is whole again, and the mind can understand. Once the mind sees the arm returned, resurrected, it can then, slowly, let it go.

After eight takes it all dissolves—I look at the screen and it isn't her at all. This isn't my house, there is no second chance, nothing, no one, is coming back. Where's my baseball glove? I ask her, and she answers sweetly, like she always does, If it was up your ass you'd know where it was. *ACTION.* We are in the kitchen, holding our breath, I am writing these notes, I am in prison, I am making a movie of being in prison, the brain can contain anything, in its little hall of mirrors. We watch the way Julianne's mouth forms the words, *I tried so hard*, though there really is only one way to say *snake*, to say *flower*, to say *gun*. But we need someone to say it to us first, to point into the cage, to point to the sky, to say the word.

*CUT.*

I finally get to change out of these wet jeans, Julianne whispers, as she passes by me. Without thinking I reach out and hug her.

THE night we filmed Dano finding De Niro sleeping beneath a bush (the imaginary night I take my father inside) was bitter cold. We did not start filming that scene until after midnight, and once De Niro was in place, wrapped in his blankets, a hat pulled down over his ears, he did not rise again, not for the three hours it took to film the scene. For the first hour the camera was on Dano, shielding his eyes with his burning palm, saying, *Hey, come on.* Then the crew worked for forty-five minutes to turn the shot around, so the camera would then be on De Niro's face (*bammo*). De Niro could have gone to his trailer between takes, he could have gotten warm, but he chose to stay on the ground, for three cold hours. For some of the takes it seemed he was actually asleep, his breath heavy, Dano standing over him, softly calling his name. With each take De Niro's face, his voice, subtly transformed, as the cold, as the earth, seeped into him.

Next fall, before the movie comes out, as the anniversary of my mother's death once again approaches, someone I hardly know will ask, Are you going to see your family over the holidays? At first I'll be confused, because all I can think is that I live with my family—Maeve, Lili—I see them every day, but then I'll realize that he's speaking of my family of origin (Mom, Dad), and I'll smile. No, I won't be seeing them this year.

● ● ○

**A** year from now, in the first few weeks after the film opens, we will do a handful of benefit screenings for various Housing First organizations. I will invite David Eagleman to the screening in Houston, and a few days afterward I will go to his lab, talk about my experience of seeing my life reenacted. I propose he hooks me up to an fMRI, study which parts of my brain light up as I watch Julianne empty her pill bottle. Will it be the same area that lights up when I see the crane shot of De Niro curling up on a heating grate for his first night sleeping rough? Will a different area light up when Dano smokes crack? As we talk I notice a dead bird on the sill outside of the window beside us. We talk about birds for a moment, how they sometimes don't see the glass. Eagleman says, In a year we will remember almost nothing of this moment.

A few months later I will give a public talk with the cognitive psychologist (William Hirst) who specializes in trauma and group memory. We are at the Rubin Museum in New York, surrounded by Buddhas. Our talk is part of a series called *Brainwave*, the focus of which is memory. One of Hirst's experiments has shown that people's memories, especially flashbulb memories (trauma, violence, death), are notoriously unreliable. At one point Hirst will propose that soon—if it hasn't happened already—whatever memory I have of my mother will be replaced by Juli-

307

anne Moore. I won't even be aware it has happened. The talk, up to this moment, has been utterly engaging, yet I can't help but laugh—I love what Julianne did, but I just don't see that happening. I'm not that far gone.

I send Eagleman a note the next day: *I still remember that bird.*

**THREE** times in our film (which ends up called *Being Flynn*) my real-life wife (Lili) will lightly touch my twenty-seven-year-old screen self (Dano)—I don't believe any of these gestures are in the script. The last time is at the end of the movie, as Dano leaves the shelter, when Lili reaches through the cage and hugs him, grabbing fistfuls of his leather jacket, as she says goodbye. Paul told Lili, before one of the takes, that she is about to go out—to relapse, on cocaine, or maybe she is already dabbling, chipping (this is her *motivation*). Maybe she holds onto Dano so tightly as a way to pull herself back from the edge of the well. The second time Lili touches Dano is when De Niro has been in the shelter for a while and has begun to act out, to cause trouble, and his behavior is being discussed in a change-of-shift meeting. As a new worker recounts the story of Dano's (my) father's erratic behavior, Dano snaps at him, *What are you looking at? This isn't me we're talking about.* Lili reaches over and touches Dano's knee ever so lightly, as if to say, *I understand*, or, *It's going to be all right.* The first touch is as Dano sits in the office, early in the movie, reading a letter my father wrote me, just days after he first showed up at the shelter, requesting a room. We hear De Niro's voice: *Writers, especially poets, are especially prone to madness.* Lili touches Dano lightly on the shoulder as she walks past, asking, *How you doing, babe?* Dano jumps, and I jump, watching it. Here is the future, tapping my younger self on the shoulder, saying, *I will be here for you, if you can find your way to me.*

# [SOME NOTES, SOME INSPIRATIONS]

## ONE

—José Saramago, *Blindness*.

(*Note*: the actual quote is: *There being no witnesses, and if there were there is no evidence that they were summoned to the post-mortems to tell us what happened, it is understandable that someone should ask how it was possible to know that these things happened so and not in some other manner, the reply to be given is that all stories are like those about the creation of the universe; no one was there, no one witnessed anything, yet everyone knows what happened.*)

—Antonio Damasio, *The Feeling of What Happens*.

—*In this it resembles*: Robert Hass, "Meditation on Lagunitas."

—V. S. Ramachandran, *A Brief Tour of Human Consciousness*.

—Anne Carson, from "Screaming in Translation," the introduction to her translation of Sophocles' *Electra*.

—Genesis 1:26.

—Franz Wright, "The Only Animal."

—Géza Vermes, *The Authentic Gospel of Jesus*.

—Pierre Teilhard de Chardin, via Annie Dillard, *For the Time Being*.

## TWO

—*Cells that fire together*: Carla Shatz (*on Hebbian learning*).

—Friedrich Nietzsche, "On the Uses and Disadvantages of History for Life," in *The Collective Memory Reader*.

## THREE

—Yasmin Anwar, "Scientists Use Brain Imaging To Reveal The Movie In Our Mind," *UC Berkeley News*, 22 September 2011.

—David Eagleman, *Incognito.*

—Virginia Woolf, *Moments of Being.*

—Stanley Kunitz, in a conversation with Mark Katzman, American Museum of Natural History, 2003.

—Marcus Raichle, "The Brain's Dark Energy," *Scientific American,* March 2010.

—Mario Livio, interviewed by Krista Tippet, *On Being,* NPR, 2011.

—*Drill one hole after another into it*: Samuel Beckett, in a letter to Axel Kaun, 9 July 1937.

## FOUR

—Nietzsche, ibid.

—Richard Dawkins, *The Selfish Gene.*

—Walter Benjamin, "The Storyteller and Theses on the Philosophy of History," in *The Collective Memory Reader.*

—Damasio, ibid.

## FIVE

—James Frey, *A Million Little Pieces* (fake memoir, sold millions).

—Margaret B. Jones, *Love and Consequences* (fake memoir, pulped).

—*It is night*: Nick Flynn (NF), "Father Outside."

—Susan Sontag, *On Photography* (1977), *Regarding the Pain of Others* (2002).

—Michael Patrick McDonald, *All Souls.*

## SIX

—Leopold Blaschka, letter to Mary Lee Ware, 1889.
(*Note*: the rest of the Glass Flower information in this chapter is from various sources, including Wikipedia.)

—*The Sistine Chapel of glasswork*: Susan Rossi-Wilcox, *ResearchPennState,* 1999.

—Joan Didion, *The Year of Magical Thinking.*

—Ernst Jentsch, "On the Psychology of the Uncanny," 1905.

## SEVEN

—Maurizio Cattelan: *All* (2007), the Menil Collection, 2010.

—*I was cheered*: W. C. Williams, "Asphodel, That Greeny Flower."

—*And god forgive me*: Denis Johnson, "Poem."

—Kevin Young, from his introduction to *The Art of Losing: Poems of Grief and Healing*.

—Paul Levy, "God and the Imagination."

## EIGHT

—Edgar Morin, "Le cinema ou l'homme imaginaire."

—Simone Weil, "To Desire Without an Object," *Gravity and Grace*.

—*To see how far*: NF, "You Ask How."
   (*Note*: the actual line is, *to know how far* . . . )

—*And the world become a bell*: NF, "Sudden."

## NINE

—*The emptiness of the bowl creates the bowl*: a basic teaching of Buddhism (see also the concept of *Interbeing*).

—Maurice Halbwachs, from *The Collective Memory*, in *The Collective Memory Reader*.

—Damasio, ibid.

—Hugh Everett III, 1930–1982 (though perhaps he still exists in a parallel universe).

—Walt Whitman, "Song of Myself."

—Henry David Thoreau, *Walden* (last paragraph).

## TEN

—Guy Maddin, *My Winnipeg*.

—*Absolute unmixed attention is prayer*: Weil, "The Allegory of the Cave."

—*If you find yourself lost*: NF, "Elsewhere, Mon Amour."

## ELEVEN

—Dr. Harold Edgerton, *.30 bullet piercing an apple*, 1964.
   (*Note*: I just found the image online, and it seems I've misremembered, all these years—both the entry and the exit of the bullet do significant damage to the apple.)

—Rebecca Solnit, "The Annihilation of Time and Space," *River of Shadows, Eadweard Muybridge and the Technological Wild West*.

## THIRTEEN

—Dr. Jim O'Connell, Boston Health Care for the Homeless Program.

—Sorites Paradox, The paradox of the grandfather's axe, the Ship of Theseus, the paradox of the heap—I was directed into these paradoxes by Tad Flynn, and all contain some information culled from Wikipedia.

—*Someday, son, this awl will be yours*: from a *New Yorker* cartoon (provenance lost).

—*like a tree learns to swallow barbed wire*: from a poem (provenance lost).

## FIFTEEN

—*Radiolab*, "The Bus Stop," 2010.

—Barry Schwabsky, "Gillian Wearing," *Artforum*, September 2000.

—*Grain upon grain*: Beckett, *Endgame*.

## SIXTEEN

—*I dream only of the orifices of the body*: Jean Genet, *A Thief's Journal*.

—*if his story were pure enough*: a riff (of course) on the Kunitz poem "King of the River" (*If the water were clear enough*).

—Damasio, *Self Comes to Mind*.

## SEVENTEEN

—AIDS Service Center New York is an empowerment agency for formerly homeless drug addicts.

—*Note*: during one take while shooting the next-to-last scene De Niro improvised a rant about "pedophilic priests"—it is this take that makes it into the film.

## NINETEEN

—*Attention must be paid*: Arthur Miller, *Death of a Salesman*.

—*The first human being captured*: Solnit, ibid.

## TWENTY

—*The practical application of the Glass Flowers*: Frances Richard, "Great Vitreous Tact," *Cabinet*, 2002.

—*Any day now I'll make a knife*: W. S. Merwin, "October."

—*Remember, no matter what*: from a taped tour of the Glass Flowers.

# [SOME NOTES, SOME INSPIRATIONS]

—Walt Whitman, "Song of Myself."
—Dew Harrison, "Christopher Williams, *Angola to Vietnam*."
—Adam Hochschild, *King Leopold's Ghost*.

## TWENTY-ONE

—*Note*: Edoardo got in touch with me shortly after I wrote that passage.
—*Of god, the Kabbalah asserts*: Annie Dillard, ibid.
—Jana Prikryl, "The Genius of Buster," *New York Review of Books*, 9 June 2011.
—Kristin Prevallet, <www.trancepoetics.com>.

## TWENTY-TWO

—*Ragin' (Full-On)* is (of course) the title of the first fIREHOSE album.

## TWENTY-THREE

—*Please do not lean on the cases*: a sign in the Glass Flowers exhibit.
—*The moment one gives close attention*: Henry Miller.
—*See the white powdery stuff on the leaves*: Rossi-Wilcox, ibid.

## TWENTY-FOUR

—René Clair, *Paris Qui Dort* (1924).
—Damon Gaugh, aka Badly Drawn Boy.
—Damasio, *Self Comes to Mind*.
—*The whole great enterprise of life*: Robert Frost, discussing "Kitty Hawk."
—*If you possess the image*: Carl Jung, *The Red Book*.
—Aristotle, *Poetics*.
—Maggie Nelson, *The Art of Cruelty*.

## TWENTY-FIVE

—"Physicists Find Elusive Particle Seen as Key to Universe," Dennis Overbye, *New York Times*, 4 July 2012.
—Eagleman, ibid.
—Alix Lambert, *Crime*.
—*Let's return to the scene*: NF, "Jesus Knew."

# [DEBTS]

**IMPOSSIBLE WITHOUT**  lili taylor   jill bialosky   bill clegg   tad
flynn   paul dano   liam broggy   julianne moore   olivia thirlby
james schamus   jane rosenthal   michael costigan   andrew
miano   dan balgoyan   joan sobel   ofe yi   caroline baron   renee
foley burke   aude bronson-howard   rufino colon   sarah knowles
joyce myricks   helen boben   monica ruiz-ziegler   joseph prio-
leau   ryan webb   robert andrews   annie tan   christo morse
badly drawn boy   edwin rivera   declan quinn   gerard sava
thomas hoffman r.i.p.   joey boots   devin donegan   stephen williams   sharen duke   jessica greer morris   aids service center nyc
susan perlman   casey madigan   tom conway   ryan heck   jerry
decarlo   teamsters/catering/cast/crew being flynn   focus fea-
tures   radioman   radiohead   radiolab   occupy wall street   yes
men   andy bichelbaum   julian assange   wikipedia   wikileaks
alison granucci   alison liss   shaun dolan   kapo amos ng   nancy
palmquist   bill rusin   dave cole   w. w. norton   jim frost   atlan-
tic center for the arts   jim harithas   station museum   bronfman
center   zack zook   rebecca schultz   chad bunning   rubin
museum   brainwave   william hirst   housing first   housing
works   eileen o'brien   elders living at home   lyndia downey
pine street inn   eddie devereaux r.i.p.   richard booton r.i.p.
ivan hubbard r.i.p.   st. francis house   sam tsemberis   jamie

318

## [DEBTS]

taylor   pathways to housing   arturo bendixen   aids foundation of chicago   bowery mission   doug montgomery   mel chin hubert sauper   cordia villacarlos   mark adams   tom johnston joyce linehan   sophie klahr   dean wareham   stephen elliott tony swofford   debra gitterman   thich nhat hanh   karen farber kelle groom   nina douglas   eduordo di angelis   d. boon r.i.p. kathleen schmieder   walter white   j kasteley   anastacia   michael stipe   sam cole   alex lemon   brooklyn writers space   captain mike   rebecca wadlinger   todd tupper   tunnel city coffee   guy maddin   beth bachmann   buster keaton   mark conway   william middleton   jesse pinkman   david eagleman   michael jamieson russ aharonian   spiritualized   samuel beckett   roscommon ronnie yates   austin havican   david shields   john d'agata   eula biss   anne carson   rebecca solnit   eric fair   marie howe   jim shepard   karen shepard   carolyn forché   maeve lulu taylor flynn
**IMPOSSIBLE WITHOUT**

**NICK FLYNN** has worked as a ship's captain, an electrician, and as a caseworker with folks who found themselves without a fixed address for a period of time (*see note below*). His film credits include field poet and artistic collaborator on *Darwin's Nightmare* (which was nominated for an Academy Award in 2006), and executive producer (collaborator) on *Being Flynn* (2012). Each spring he teaches poetry, nonfiction, and collaboration at the University of Houston—the rest of the year he is in, or near, Brooklyn.

*note*: I used to say I worked as *a caseworker with the homeless*, but I've come to believe that the term *homeless* has a stereotype (and therefore violence) built into it. From now on I'm going to try to use either *the working poor* or *folks who found themselves without a fixed address* (the French use the term *SDF—sans domicile fixe*) *for a period of time*.